GeeKCHIC CROCHET

GEEKCHICCROCHET

35 retro-inspired projects that are off the hook

NICKI TRENCH

CICO BOOKS
LONDON NEW YORK

Published in 2012 by CICO Books
an imprint of Ryland Peters & Small Ltd
519 Broadway, 5th Floor, New York, NY 10012

www.cicobooks.com

10 9 8 7 6 5 4 3 2 1

A CIP catalogue record for this book is available from the
Library of Congress.

ISBN: 978 1 908862 05 1

Printed in China

Editor: Marie Clayton
Designer: Alison Fenton
Photographer: Penny Wincer
Stylist: Rob Merrett
Technique illustrations: Stephen Dew and Kate Simunek

For digital editions, visit www.cicobooks.com/apps.php

CONTENTS

INTRODUCTION

Crochet fashion has certainly hit the fashion catwalk runways and *Geek Chic Crochet* brings you 35 vintage-style garments and accessories patterns to hand crochet. There is a huge revival in '70s and '80s styles and the designs in this book are inspired by hippy, boho, festival-chic fashion that is just everywhere right now. Not since the crochet explosion of the '60s has crochet caught everyone's attention.

When researching this book, I have taken many enjoyable trips to Brick Lane, a trendy and fashionable area in east London, full of vintage shops, art galleries, and cafes. Here you can find a young, art-school sense of fashion and spot the sometimes outlandish dress styles worn by many of its inhabitants; this may not be totally represented here, but I've tried to bring elements of this fashion into the designs and colors and hope that these will entice you into making the projects yourself.

This book has an excellent illustrated techniques section to guide you through the stitches and I've tried to keep the pattern terminology as straightforward as possible. Each pattern has been categorized into three sections of ability: Beginner, Improver, or Experienced. Even the simplest pattern will have you drooling; take a look at the Chunky Patchwork Scarf on page 32 or the Tie on page 18—these are two of the very simplest patterns to follow, but will have you running for your crochet hook. If you prefer more of a challenge, look at the Slouch Bag on page 104 or have a go at the Fur-collared Cardigan on page 64.

There are plenty of patterns for the Improver level too—look at the Peter Pan Collar Cardigan on page 72 and the Tweed Skirt on page 88.

If you have not considered crochet as fashionable, now is the time to have a rethink… so get your hooks and yarn out and join the crochet revival—you won't be disappointed.

Tie

Lacy Collar

Beanie Hat
Turban Headband
Neckerchief
Ribbon Hat
Tie
Hair Bow
Tassel Earrings
Lacy Collar
Cloche Hat

HEAD & SHOULDERS

Ribbon Hat

Hair Bow

Neckerchief

Cloche Hat

A MUST-HAVE BASIC BEANIE HAT, CROCHETED IN A SUPERSOFT BABY ALPACA AND MERINO WOOL MIX THAT LOOKS AND FEELS GREAT.

BEANIE HAT

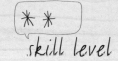

skill level

MATERIALS

50% baby alpaca/50% merino mix sport (babyweight) yarn, such as Rooster Almerino Baby
>> 2 x 1¾oz (50g) balls—approx 274yd (250m)—of blue-green

US size E/4 (3.5mm) crochet hook

Abbreviations
ch chain
hdc half double crochet
hdc2tog half double crochet 2 stitches together
rep repeat
RS right side
sc single crochet
ss slip stitch
st(s) stitch(es)
WS wrong side

Gauge
18 sts x 14 rows over 4in. (10cm) square working hdc using US size E/4 (3.5mm) hook.

Size
One size.

Finished measurement
7in. (18cm) deep x 19¾in. (50cm) circumference.

Hat

Make 90ch, join with ss in first ch to form a ring.

Round 1: 1ch, skip st at base of ch, 1sc in each ch, join with ss in first ch. (90 sts)

Round 2: 1ch, skip st at base of ch, 1sc in each st, join with ss in first ch.

Rounds 3–12: Rep Round 2.

Round 13: 2ch, skip st at base of ch, 1hdc in each st to end, join with ss in top of first 2-ch.

Rounds 14–24: Rep Round 13.

Round 25: 2ch, skip st at base of ch, *1hdc in each of next 9 sts, hdc2tog; rep from * to last st, 1hdc in last st, join with ss in top of first 2-ch. (82 sts)

Round 26: Rep Round 13.

Round 27: 2ch, skip st at base of ch, 1hdc in each of next 8 sts, hdc2tog; rep from * to last st, 1hdc in last st, join with ss in top of first 2-ch. (74 sts)

Round 28: Rep Round 13.

Round 29: 2ch, skip st at base of ch, *1hdc in each of next 7 sts, hdc2tog; rep from * to last st, 1hdc in last st, join with ss in top of first 2-ch. (66 sts)

Round 30: 2ch, skip st at base of ch, *1hdc in each of next 6 sts, hdc2tog; rep from * to last st, 1hdc in last st, join with ss in top of first 2-ch. (58 sts)

Round 31: 2ch, skip st at base of ch, *1hdc in each of next 5 sts, hdc2tog; rep from * to last st, 1hdc in last st, join with ss in top of first 2-ch. (50 sts)

Round 32: 2ch, skip st at base of ch, *1hdc in each of next 4 sts, hdc2tog; rep from * to last st, 1hdc in last st, join with ss in top of first 2-ch. (42 sts)

Round 33: 2ch, skip st at base of ch, *1hdc in each of next 3 sts, hdc2tog; rep from * to last st, 1hdc in last st, join with ss in top of first 2-ch. (34 sts)

Fasten off leaving a tail of approx 8in. (20cm).

Finishing

Working on WS of hat and using yarn needle, thread tail and insert needle through top of each st at top of hat, pull tightly to close hole, and fasten off. Allow brim to roll up on RS.

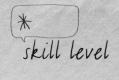

skill level

A REALLY QUICK AND EASY PROJECT, THIS HEADBAND IS IDEAL FOR BEGINNERS. IT CAN BE MADE IN A COUPLE OF HOURS, KEEPS YOU WARM, AND IS A LOT LESS BULKY THAN A THICK HAT.

TURBAN HEADBAND

MATERIALS

100% Peruvian highland wool light worsted (DK) yarn, such as Cascade 220
>> 1 x 3½oz (100g) hank—approx 220yd (200m)—of turquoise

US size G/6 (4mm) crochet hook

Abbreviations
ch chain
hdc half double crochet
rep repeat
RS right side
ss slip stitch
st(s) stitch(es)
WS wrong side

Gauge
16 sts x 10 rows over 4in. (10cm) square working hdc using US size G/6 (4mm) hook.

Size
One size.

Finished measurement
19½ x 3¾in. (49 x 9.5cm).

Headband

Make 17ch.
Row 1: 1hdc in 2nd ch from hook, 1hdc in each ch to end. (15 sts)
Row 2: 2ch, 1hdc in each st to end.
Rep Row 2 until work measures approx 19½in. (49cm) or to fit around head.
Fasten off.

Front Tie

Make 10ch.
Row 1: 1hdc in 2nd ch from hook. (9 sts)
Row 2: 2ch, 1hdc in each st to end.
Rep Row 2 until work measures approx 3½in. (9cm).
Fasten off.

Finishing

Fold in headband half so short ends meet, with RS together.
Join together with ss seam. Turn RS out.
Wrap tie around headband and join seam ends of tie with ss seam, making sure seam is on WS of headband.

neckerchief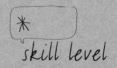

skill level

I'VE USED A COMBINATION OF DIFFERENT THICKNESS YARNS HERE, CHOSEN FOR COLOR AND TEXTURE. AND I'VE ADDED THE SIMPLEST EDGING, SO IT'S A SUITABLE PROJECT FOR A BEGINNER—BUT FEEL FREE TO ADD ANY EDGING YOU LIKE.

MATERIALS

50% baby alpaca/50% merino mix light worsted (DK) yarn, such as Rooster Almerino DK

» 1 x 1¾oz (50g) ball—approx 124yd (112.5m)—of off-white

» ¼ x 1¾oz (50g) ball—approx 31yd (30m)—of yellow

50% baby alpaca/50% merino wool mix worsted (Aran) yarn, such as Rooster Almerino Aran

» ¼ x 1¾oz (50g) ball—approx 26yd (25m)—each of blue, coral

50% baby alpaca/50% merino mix sport (babyweight) yarn, such as Rooster Almerino Baby

» ¼ x 1¾oz (50g) ball—approx 34yd (31m)—of pale green

80% baby alpaca/20% silk mix laceweight yarn, such as Rooster Delightful Lace

» ¹⁄₁₆ x 3½oz (100g) hank—approx 52yd (50m)—of dark red

76% super kid mohair/24% silk lace laceweight yarn, such as Debbie Bliss Angel

» ¼ x ⅞oz (25g) ball—approx 55yd (50m)—each of green-blue, bright pink, green, orange

55% merino/33% microfiber/12% cashmere light worsted (DK) yarn, such as Debbie Bliss Cashmerino DK

» ¼ x 1¾oz (50g) ball—approx 30yd (28m)—of navy

60% cupro/40% polyester metallic yarn, such as Rowan Shimmer

» ¼ x ⅞oz (25g) ball—approx 46yd (44m)—of silver

US size E/4 (3.5mm) crochet hook

Abbreviations

ch chain
cont continue
dc double crochet
hdc half double crochet
rep repeat
RS right side
sc single crochet
st(s) stitch(es)
tr treble
WS wrong side

Gauge

17 sts over 4in. (10cm) working hdc using US size E/4 (3.5mm) hook—row gauge is not important for this design.

Finished measurement

14in. (36cm) deep x 17¾in. (45cm) across top edge.

Neckerchief

Using first color, make 2ch, 2sc in 2nd ch from hook. (2 sts)

Row 1: 1ch, 2sc in each st. (4 sts)

Row 2 (WS): 1ch, 2sc in first st, 1sc in each of next 2 sts, 2sc in last st.

Cont in stripes of 1, 2, or 3 rows of hdc, using colors randomly.

Next row: 2ch, 1hdc in first st, 1hdc in each st to last st, 2hdc in top of turning ch.

Rep last row until work measures 11¾in. (30cm), ending with a RS row.

Fasten off.

Top Edging

Using MC, make 90ch (first tie).

Row 1 (WS): Join ch to right-hand corner of top edge (first tie), make 1sc in each st along top, make 90ch (2nd tie).

Row 2 (RS): 1sc in 2nd ch from hook and in each ch to top edge, 1sc in each st along top edge, 1sc in each ch to end of second tie.

Row 3 (WS): 1ch, 1sc in first st, *2ch, skip next 2 sts, 1sc in next st; rep from * to end.

Row 4 (RS): 1ch, * [1sc, 1ch, 1hdc, 1ch, 1dc, 1ch, 1tr, 1ch] in next ch loop, 1tr in next sc, 1ch, [1tr, 1ch, 1dc, 1ch, 1hdc, 1ch, 1sc] in next loop, 1sc in next sc; rep from * to end.

Fasten off.

Side Edging

Row 1: With WS facing, join MC at top left edge. Work sc along length to tip, 3sc in tip, work sc along 2nd side to top edge.

Row 2 (RS): 1ch, 1sc in each st along first side, 3sc in tip, 1sc in each st along 2nd side.

Row 3 (WS): 1ch, 1sc in first st, *2ch, skip next 2 sts, 1sc in next st; rep from * to end.

Row 4 (RS): 1ch, * [1sc, 1ch, 1hdc, 1ch, 1dc, 1ch, 1tr, 1ch] in next ch loop, 1tr in next sc, 1ch, [1tr, 1ch, 1dc, 1ch, 1hdc, 1ch, 1sc] in next loop, 1sc in next sc; rep from * to end.

Fasten off.

Finishing

Sew in ends and block.

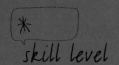
RIBBON HAT

A FUN, EASY HAT THAT CAN BE DRESSED UP WITH A LENGTH OF PRETTY RIBBON, BRAIDED YARN, OR LOVELY VINTAGE FABRIC.

Abbreviations
ch chain
dc double crochet
hdc half double crochet
rep repeat
ss slip stitch
st(s) stitch(es)

Special abbreviations
fpdc
(front post double)
dc worked around stalk
of st from previous
round from front of work
bpdc
(back post double)
dc worked around stalk of st from previous
round from back of work

Gauge
15 sts x 12 rows over 4in. (10cm) square
working hdc using US size G/6 (4mm) hook.

Size
One size.

Finished measurement
10in. (25.5cm) deep x 20in. (51cm)
circumference.

Tip
Post stitches are worked around the stalk of the stitch from the previous round and not into the top of the stitch. When worked as in this pattern, alternating front and back post stitches, they result in a rib at the brim of the hat.

MATERIALS
50% baby alpaca/50% merino mix light worsted (DK) yarn, such as Rooster Almerino DK
» 2 x 1¾oz (50g) balls—approx 248yd (225m)—of dark gray

US size G/6 (4mm) crochet hook

40in. (1m) of ½-in. (12-mm) wide ribbon

Hat
Make 76ch, join with ss in first ch to form a ring.
Round 1: 3ch (counts as 1dc here and throughout), 1dc in each ch, join with ss in top of 3-ch. (76 dc)
Round 2: 3ch, skip first st, *fpdc around stalk of next dc from Round 1, bpdc around stalk of next dc; rep from * to end, fpdc around stalk of last dc, join with ss in top of 3-ch.
Round 3: Rep Round 2.
Round 4: 2ch, skip first st, 1hdc in each st to end, join with ss in top of 2-ch.
Rounds 5–25: Rep Round 4.
Round 26 (eyelet round): 3ch, skip next st, *1hdc in each of next 3 sts, 1ch, skip next st; rep from * to last 2 sts, 1hdc in each of last 2 sts, join with ss in 2nd ch of 3-ch.
Round 27: 2ch, *1hdc in ch-1 sp, 1hdc in each of next 3 sts; rep from * to end omitting 1hdc at end of last rep, join with ss in top of 2-ch.
Rounds 28–31: 2ch, 1hdc in each st to end, join with ss in top of 2-ch.
Fasten off.

Finishing
Sew in all ends. Weave ribbon through eyelet round.

CROCHET AND KNITTED TIES ARE THE HEIGHT OF FASHION! THIS IS A VERY SIMPLE PATTERN AND MAKES A REALLY COOL MAN'S ACCESSORY.

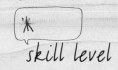

skill level

TIE

Tie

Make 10ch.

Row 1: 1hdc in 3rd ch from hook, 1hdc in each of next 7 ch.

Row 2: 2ch (counts as 1hdc), 1hdc in each st to end, 1hdc in top of 2-ch from previous row. (9 sts)

Rep Row 2 until tie measures approx 55in. (140cm) or length required.

Fasten off.

Finishing

Sew in ends.

Block and press lightly, using a damp cloth.

MATERIALS

100% cotton 4-ply crochet thread, such as DMC Natura Just Cotton

>> 1 x 1¾oz (50g) ball—approx 170yd (155m)—of red

US size C/2 (2.5mm) crochet hook

Abbreviations	Gauge	Size
ch chain	22 sts x 15 rows over	One size.
hdc half double crochet	4in. (10cm) square working hdc using US	
rep repeat	size C/2 (2.5mm)	**Finished measurement**
st(s) stitch(es)	hook.	1½in. (4cm) wide x 55in. (140cm) long.

VERY CUTE, VERY EASY, VERY BRIGHT!
MAKE LOTS OF HAIR BOWS IN A
RANGE OF CANDY COLORS.

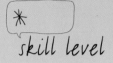

skill level

HAIR BOW

MATERIALS

100% cotton 4-ply crochet thread, such as DMC Natura
Just Cotton

>> 1 x 1¾oz (50g) ball—approx 170yd (155m)—each
of lilac, coral, red, aquamarine

US size D/3 (3mm) crochet hook

Abbreviations

ch chain
hdc half double crochet
sc single crochet
st(s) stitch(es)
WS wrong side

Gauge

17 sts x 15 rows over 4in.
(10cm) square working
hdc using US size D/3
(3mm) hook.

Finished measurement

4½ x 2⅛in. (11.5 x 5.5cm).

Main Bow

Make 42ch.
Row 1: 1hdc in 3rd ch from hook, 1hdc in each ch to end. (40 sts)
Rows 2–8: 1ch, 1hdc in each st to end.
Fasten off.

Middle Bar

Make 15ch.
Row 1: 1sc in 2nd ch from hook and in each ch to end. (14 sts)
Rows 2–6: 1ch, 1sc in each st to end. (13 sts)
Fasten off.

Finishing

Fold two ends of main bow into center, WS together, and sew ends
together while gathering up slightly. Sew in ends.
Take middle bar and fold over main bow center, sewing ends together on
WS. Sew in ends.

Tip

Try using different colors for the bow and
middle bar to really make them stand out.

I LOVE THESE EARRINGS—THEY ARE SO COOL AND EASY TO MAKE. ALTHOUGH NOT STRICTLY CROCHET, A CROCHET HOOK IS USED TO MAKE THEM.

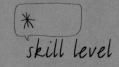

skill level

TASSEL EARRINGS

Earrings

Step 1: Cut a whole skein of embroidery floss in half, keeping the paper wrapper on each half toward the looped end to hold the strands in place while you are assembling the earring.

Step 2: Carefully pull 2 strands away from one half and set aside. Push a crochet hook through all the loops at one end to hold the bundle in position.

Step 3: Tie the looped end firmly just below the crochet hook, using the 2 strands and a double knot. Thread a tapestry needle with the ends and pass it twice through the tie to secure, then trim the loose ends close to the knot.

Step 4: Remove the crochet hook and the paper wrapper. Open the jump ring with some small household pliers and thread all the loops into the ring.

Step 5: Hook the ring of the fish hook earring finding onto the jump ring. Close the jump ring tightly.

Rep Steps 2–5 to make other earring.

Finishing

Trim the lengths of floss to an even length, if necessary.

Tip

If you need earrings in an emergency, just keep the elements in stock and you can assemble a pair in no time to match your outfit. They also make fantastic gifts for friends.

MATERIALS

1 skein of embroidery floss per pair of earrings

Crochet hook

Tapestry needle

2 silver-plated 9mm jump rings per pair of earrings

2 silver-plated fish hook earring findings per pair of earrings

Size
One size.

A STYLISH COLLAR FOR A BLOUSE OR SWEATER MAKES
AN EXQUISITE AND UNIQUE GIFT. IT'S EASY TO MAKE
ONCE YOU GET USED TO A TINY HOOK AND FINE YARN.

* * *
skill level

LACY COLLAR

MATERIALS
No. 30 100% cotton 6-ply crochet
thread, such as DMC Cordonnet
>> 1 x ¾oz (20g) ball—approx 198m
(216yd)—of white

US size 10 (1.25mm) steel
crochet hook

Abbreviations
ch chain
cont continue
dc double crochet
dtr double treble
patt pattern
rem remaining
RS right side
sc single crochet
sp(s) space(s)
ss slip stitch
st(s) stitch(es)
tr treble
trtr triple treble
WS wrong side

Special abbreviation
picot
4ch, 1sc in 4th ch from
hook (1 picot made)

Gauge
On Row 4, 2 repeats of
patt measure 1½in. (4cm)
across using US size 10
(1.25mm) hook.

Size
One size.

Finished measurement
Neck edge 9½in. (24cm)
3½in. (6.5cm) deep

Collar
(make 2 pieces the same)
Make 59ch.
Row 1: 1sc in 3rd ch from hook, *5ch, skip 3 ch,
1sc in next ch; rep from * to end. (14 sps)
Row 2: 3ch, 1sc in 3rd of 5-ch, *5ch, 1sc in 3rd of
next 5-ch; rep from * ending 3ch, 1dc in last sc.
Row 3: 5ch, *[3dtr, picot, 3dtr] in 3rd of next 5-ch,
2ch, 1sc in 3rd of next 5-ch, 2ch; rep from * ending
[3dtr, picot, 3dtr] in 3rd of last 5-ch, 1dtr in 3rd of 3-ch.
Row 4: 4ch, 1sc in first picot, *2ch, [3dtr, picot, 3dtr]
in next sc, 2ch, 1sc in next picot; rep from * ending
with 1tr in 5th of first 5-ch.
Row 5: 6ch, 1sc in first picot, *2ch, [3dtr, picot, 3dtr]
in next sc, 2ch, 1sc in next picot; rep from * ending
with 1trtr in last sc.
Rep Row 5 3 more times.
Row 9: 6ch, 1sc in first picot, 2ch, [3dtr, picot, 3dtr] in
next sc, 2ch, 1sc in last picot, 1trtr in last sc.
Fasten off.

Neck edging

Join thread to first foundation ch of one piece and (working on other side of ch) work 1sc in each foundation ch. At end of foundation ch, join in 2nd piece and cont to work 1sc in each foundation ch of 2nd piece (this joins both pieces together).
Fasten off.

Edging

Row 1: Work a row of sps (5ch, 1sc), 16 sps outside and 15 sps inside on each point, omitting 5ch between sc at join of points, turn.

Row 2: *5ch, 1sc in 3rd of 5-ch (picot made), 2ch, 1sc in 3rd of 5-ch of Row 1; rep from * around point, ending 1sc in 3rd of 5-ch of last sp of first point. Commence next point with 1sc in 3rd of 5-ch of first sp, rep from * to end of 2nd point ending with ss in foundation ch.
Fasten off.

Finishing

Block and press.

THIS PRETTY HAT IS MADE BY JOINING
FLOWER MOTIFS; IT WAS INSPIRED BY A
VINTAGE PATTERN OVER 50 YEARS OLD!

skill level

CLOCHE HAT

MATERIALS

50% baby alpaca/50% merino mix sport (babyweight)
yarn, such as Rooster Almerino Baby

>> 2 x 1¾oz (50g) balls—approx 274yd (250m)—of
off-white (A)
>> 1 x 1¾oz (50g) ball—approx 137yd (125m)—each
of pink (B), dark pink (C)

US size D/3 (3mm) crochet hook

Abbreviations

ch chain
dc double crochet
hdc half double
    crochet
rep repeat
sc single crochet
sp space
ss slip stitch
st(s) stitch(es)
WS wrong side

Special abbreviation

picot

6ch, ss in 4th ch from
hook (1 picot made)

Gauge

Motif measures 5in.
(12.5cm) square.

Size

One size.

Finished measurement

19¾in. (50cm)
circumference.

Top Motif

Using A, make 6ch, ss in first ch to form a ring.

Round 1: 1ch, 16sc in ring, join with ss in first sc.

Round 2: 1ch, 1sc in first st, *3ch, skip next st, 1sc in next st; rep from
* 6 times more, 3ch, join with ss in first sc.

Round 3: [1sc, 5dc, 1sc] in each 3-ch sp to end; pull first petal toward you,
1sc in first sc of Round 2. (8 petals)

Round 4: Working behind petals, *4ch, 1sc in next sc of Round 2; rep from
* ending 4ch, join with ss in sc at end of Round 3.

Round 5: [1sc, 5dc, 1sc] in each 4-ch sp to end, 1sc in sc at end of Round 3.

Round 6: Working behind petals, *5ch, 1sc in next sc of Round 4; rep from
* ending 5ch, join with a ss in sc at end of Round 5.

Round 7: [1sc, 7dc, 1sc] in each 5-ch sp to end, join with a ss in sc at end
of Round 5.

Round 8: *[picot twice, 2ch (picot loop made), 1sc in next sp between
petal] twice, picot 3 times, 2ch, 1sc in same sp between petals, (corner
loop made); rep from * 3 times.

Round 9: Ss in each st of first loop to center of loop between 2 picots, 1ch,
1sc in loop, *picot twice, 2ch, 1sc in center of next loop between 2 picots,
picot twice, 2ch, 1sc in next corner loop between first and second picots,
work a corner loop working the sc in same corner loop between 2nd and
3rd picots, picot twice, 2ch, 1sc in center of next loop; rep from * around
ending ss in first sc.
Fasten off.

Side Motif

(make 4)

Using B, work as top motif to end of Round 4.

Change to C and work Rounds 5–7.

Change to A and work Round 8.

Round 9 (joining round): Ss in each st of first loop to center of loop between 2 picots, 1ch, 1sc in loop, picot twice, 2ch, 1sc in center of next loop, picot twice, 2ch, 1sc in corner loop between first and 2nd picots, *picot, 4ch, drop loop off hook; insert hook in center picot at corner of top motif (from front to back), pick up dropped loop and join with ss through picot, 2ch, ss in 4th ch from hook (on side motif) to complete picot, picot, 2ch, 1sc in same corner loop of side motif between 2nd and 3rd picots*, [picot, 2ch, ss in center of next loop of top motif, (from back to front) picot, 2ch, 1sc in next loop of side motif] twice, picot, 2ch, ss in center of next loop on top motif, picot, 2ch, 1sc in corner loop of side motif between first and 2nd picots; rep from * to *, then complete Round as Round 9 of top motif.

Fasten off.

Work 2 more side motifs, joining to one side of top motif and to one side of previous side motif on Round 9.

Work 1 more side motif joining to top motif, 3rd side motif, and first side motif.

Edging

With WS facing, join A with 1sc in corner picot join at lower edge.

Round 1: *[5ch, 1sc in center of next loop] 3 times, 5ch, 1sc in next picot join; rep from * around, join with ss in first ch.

Round 2: [1sc, 7dc, 1sc] in each loop to end, join with ss in first sc.

Fasten off.

Finishing

Sew in ends.

Tip

The edging is worked with WS facing, so that the shells don't curl outward.

Poncho

Cowl

Vintage Lace Gloves

WINTER WALKS

Chunky Patchwork Scarf

Long Socks

Poncho
Chunky Patchwork Scarf
Cowl
Wave-&-Chevron Chunky Scarf
Vintage Lace Gloves
Long Socks

Wave-&-Chevron
Chunky Scarf

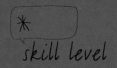
A CONTEMPORARY TWIST ON A TRADITIONAL
PONCHO MADE IN A STRAIGHTFORWARD STITCH;
BLACK HIGHLIGHTS THE BRIGHT STRIPES BETWEEN.

PONCHO

MATERIALS

100% Peruvian highland wool light worsted (DK) yarn, such as Cascade 220

» 2 x 3½oz (100g) hanks—approx 440yd (402m)—of turquoise

» 3 x 3½oz (100g) hanks—approx 660yd (603m)—of black

50% baby alpaca/50% merino mix light worsted (DK) yarn, such as Rooster Almerino DK

» 2 x 1¾oz (50g) balls—approx 248yd (225m)—of yellow

» 3 x 1¾oz (50g) balls—approx 372yd (337.5m)—each of off-white, green

» 6 x 1¾oz (50g) balls—approx 744yd (675m)—of orange

US size E/4 (3.5mm) crochet hook

Abbreviations

alt alternate
ch chain
cont continue
hdc half double crochet
hdc2tog half double crochet
  2 stitches together
rem remaining
RS right side
sc single crochet
sc2tog single crochet 2 stitches
  together

ss slip stitch
st(s) stitch(es)
tog together
WS wrong side

Gauge

17 sts x 13 rows over 4in. (10cm)
square working hdc using US size
E/4 (3.5mm) hook.

Size

One size.

Finished measurements

27in. (69cm) long x
40¼in. (102cm) wide.

Tip

Make both front and back the same, using random stripes in a mixture of different colors. Here we have mostly used a row of black to outline each color. Work between 1 and 5 rows of each color at a time.

Front & Back

(make 2 the same)

Make 175ch.

Row 1: 1hdc in 2nd ch from hook, 1hdc in each ch to end.
(174 sts)

Row 2: 2ch (counts as 1hdc), 1hdc in each st to end. (174 sts)

Cont to work in hdc until work measures 22in. (56cm).

Divide for neck.

Neck side 1:

Row 1: 2ch (counts as 1hdc), 1hdc in each of next 86 sts.
(87 sts)

Row 2: 2ch, tog (neck edge), 1hdc in each st to end.
(86 sts)

Row 3: 2ch, 1hdc in each st to last 2 sts, hdc2tog (neck edge).
(85 sts)

Rep Rows 2 and 3 (dec on neck edge only) until 74 sts rem.

Work 3 rows even.

Fasten off.

Neck side 2:

Work side 2 to match side 1, reversing shaping.

Fasten off.

Finishing

With WS together, join shoulder seams, turn RS out.

Neck edging:

Round 1: With RS facing, join turquoise in left shoulder seam at neck edge. Work sc evenly along left side to base of V, sc2tog at point of V, work sc evenly along right side to right shoulder seam. Work sc evenly along next side to base of V, sc2tog at point of V, work sc evenly along next side, join with ss in first sc.

Rounds 2–3: 1ch, make 1sc in each st to base of V, sc2tog at point of V, work 1sc in each st to base of next V, sc2tog at point of V, 1sc in each st to end, join with ss in first sc.

Fasten off and sew in ends.

For fringe, cut cream yarn into 6-½in. (16-cm) lengths and knot 3 strands tog into alt sts along lower edge of front and back.

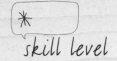

skill level *

AN OUTRAGEOUSLY LONG,
CHUNKY, BRIGHT SCARF
FOR INSTANT STYLE!

CHUNKY PATCHWORK SCARF

MATERIALS

55% merino/33% microfiber/12% cashmere worsted
(Aran) yarn, such as Debbie Bliss Cashmerino Aran

» 4 x 1¾oz (50g) balls—approx 394yd (360m)—of
black (MC)

50% baby alpaca/50% merino wool worsted (Aran)
yarn, such as Rooster Almerino Aran

» 2 x 1¾oz (50g) balls—approx 206yd (188m)—of
off-white

» 1 x 1¾oz (50g) ball—approx 94m (103yd)—each of
red, pale blue, blue-green, coral, bright pink, yellow,
pale beige, green, pale lilac, dark blue

US size H/8 (5mm) crochet hook

Abbreviations
ch chain
dc double crochet
MC main color
rep repeat
RS right side
sc single crochet
sp(s) space(s)
ss slip stitch

Gauge
Square measures 6in.
(15cm) each way when
worked using US size
H/8 (5mm) hook.

Size
One size.

Finished
measurement
118 x 12in. (300 x 30cm).

Note
Use 4 colors at random in
Rounds 1, 2, 3, & 4,
occasionally using same
color for Rounds 2 & 4, 1
& 4, or 2 & 3. Always use
MC in Round 5.

Scarf Square

(make 40)
Using first color, make 4ch, join with ss to form a ring.
Round 1: 3ch, 2dc in ring, 2ch, *[3dc, 2ch] in ring; rep from * twice more
(4 dc groups), join with ss in top of first 3-ch.
Fasten off first color.
With RS facing, join 2nd color in any 2-ch sp.
Round 2: 3ch, [2dc, 2ch, 3dc] in same ch sp, *1ch, [3dc, 2ch, 3dc] in next
ch sp; rep from * twice more, 1ch, join with ss in top of first 3-ch.
Fasten off 2nd color.
With RS facing, join 3rd color in next 2-ch sp (corner).
Round 3: 3ch, [2dc, 2ch, 3dc] in same ch sp, *1ch, 3dc in next ch sp, 1ch,
[3dc, 2ch, 3dc] in next ch sp (corner); rep from * twice more, 1ch, 3dc in
next ch sp, 1ch, join with ss in top of first 3-ch.
Fasten off 3rd color.
With RS facing, join 4th color in next 2-ch sp (corner).
Round 4: 3ch, [2dc, 2ch, 3dc] in same ch sp, *[1ch, 3dc in next ch sp]
twice, 1ch, [3dc, 2ch, 3dc] in next ch sp (corner); rep from * twice more,
[1ch, 3dc in next ch sp] twice, 1ch, join with ss in top of first 3-ch.
Fasten off 4th color.
With RS facing, join MC in next 2-ch sp (corner).
Round 5: 3ch, [2dc, 2ch, 3dc] in same ch sp (corner), *[1ch, 3dc in next ch
sp] 3 times in each of next 3 ch sps, 1ch, [3dc, 2ch, 3dc] in next ch sp
(corner); rep from * twice more, [1ch, 3dc in next ch sp] 3 times, 1ch, join
with ss in top of first 3-ch.
Fasten off, sew in ends.

Finishing

Join squares together in 20 rows of 2 with a sc seam. Sew in ends.

A NO-FUSS PROJECT, EASY TO WEAR AND MAKE. THIS
COWL IS IN A VERY SOFT YARN AND SIMPLE HALF
DOUBLES, SO CAN EASILY BE MADE IN A DAY OR TWO.

skill level # COWL

MATERIALS

50% baby alpaca/50% merino mix light worsted
(DK) yarn, such as Rooster Almerino DK

» 1 x 1¾oz (50g) ball—approx 124yd (112.5m)—
each of dark gray, off-white, red, yellow,
pale blue

US size G/5 (4mm) crochet hook

Abbreviations

ch chain
hdc half double crochet
rep repeat
sc single crochet
st(s) stitch(es)

Gauge

16 sts x 13 rows over 4in.
(10cm) square working hdc
using US size G/6 (4mm)
hook.

Size

One size.

Finished measurement

9in. (23cm) deep x 32¼in.
(82cm) circumference.

Cowl

Using first color, make 133ch.
Row 1: 1hdc in 3rd ch from hook, 1hdc in each ch to end.
Fasten off first color, attach next color.
Row 2: 2ch, skip first st, 1hdc in each st to end, 1hdc in 2nd of 2-ch.
Rep Row 2, changing color for each row, until work measures 9in. (23cm).
Fasten off.

Finishing

Join two short edges with either a sc seam or overstitch.
Sew in ends.

WAVE-&-CHEVRON CHUNKY SCARF

skill level

THIS LOVELY PATTERN RESEMBLES A FAIR-ISLE STITCH. THESE COLORS LOOK GREAT TOGETHER, BUT EXPERIMENT WITH WHATEVER COLORS SUIT YOU.

MATERIALS

50% baby alpaca/50% merino wool mix worsted (Aran) yarn, such as Rooster Almerino Aran

» 4 x 1¾oz (50g) balls—approx 412yd (376m)—of deep blue (A)

» 2 x 1¾oz (50g) balls—approx 206yd (188m)—each of red (B), yellow (C)

55% merino/33% microfiber/12% cashmere worsted (Aran) yarn, such as Debbie Bliss Cashmerino Aran

» 1 x 1¾oz (50g) ball—approx 98.5yd (90m)—of black (D)

US size G/7 (4.5mm) crochet hook

Abbreviations

beg beginning
ch chain
dc double crochet
foll following
hdc half double crochet
patt pattern
rep repeat
RS right side
sc single crochet
sc2tog single crochet 2 stitches together
sc3tog single crochet 3 stitches together
ss slip stitch
st(s) stitch(es)
tr treble
tr2tog treble 2 stitches together
tr3tog treble 3 stitches together

Gauge

14 sts x 11 rows over 4in. (10cm) square working Wave-&-Chevron patt using US size G/7 (4.5mm) hook.

Finished measurement

Approx 92½ x 7½in. (235 x 19cm).

Scarf

Using A, make 25ch.

Row 1 (RS): 1sc in 2nd ch from hook, 1sc in each ch to end. (24 sts)

Row 2: 1ch, skip 1 st, *1hdc in next st, 1dc in foll st, 3tr in next st, 1dc in foll st, 1hdc in next st, 1sc in foll st; rep from * ending last 1sc in 1-ch.

Row 3: Attach B, skip first st, 1sc in each of next 3 sts, 3sc in next st (center of 3-tr), 1sc in each of next 2 sts, *sc3tog, 1sc in each of next 2 sts, 3sc in next st, 1sc in each of next 2 sts; rep from * to last st, sc2tog over last hdc and 1-ch from previous row.

Row 4: Attach C, skip first st, 1sc in each of next 3 sts, *3sc in next st (center of 3-sc), 1sc in each of next 2 sts, sc3tog, 1sc in each of next 2 sts; rep from * to last 2 sts, sc2tog.

Row 5: Attach A, 3ch, skip first st, 1tr in next st, 1dc in foll st, *1hdc in next st, 1sc in foll st, 1hdc in next st, 1dc in foll st, tr3tog, 1dc in next st; rep from * to last 2 sts, tr2tog.

Row 6: Attach C, skip 1 st, 1sc in each st to end, ending 1sc in last tr. (24 sts)

Row 7: Attach D, skip 1 st, 1sc in each st, ending 1sc in 1-ch. (24 sts)

Row 8: Attach B, skip 1 st, 1sc in each st, ending 1sc in 1-ch. (24 sts)

Rep Rows 2–8 until work measures approx 94in. (235cm), ending on a Row 5. Fasten off.

Edging

With RS facing, attach A at beg of one long side, 1ch, work sc evenly along side, join with ss in corner st.
Fasten off.
Rep on other long side.

Finishing

Sew in ends.

DELICATE AND VINTAGE, THESE GLOVES ARE MADE IN FINE
COTTON AND REQUIRE PATIENCE—BUT ARE WORTH THE
EFFORT BECAUSE THEY MAKE AN ELEGANT ACCESSORY.

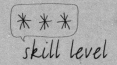
*** *
skill level

VINTAGE LACE GLOVES

MATERIALS

No. 40 100% cotton 6-ply crochet thread, such as
DMC Cordonnet

>> 2 x ¾oz (20g) balls—approx 498yd (456m)—of
white or off-white

US size 12 (1mm) steel crochet hook

20in. (50cm) fine round elastic

Yarn sewing needle

Abbreviations	Special abbreviation	Gauge
ch chain	**Popcorn**	22 dc x 20 rows over
ch sp chain space	(popcorn for main	4in. (10cm) square
cont continue	body) 5dc in next sp,	using a size US size
dc double crochet	remove hook from	12 (1mm) steel
hdc half double	loop, insert hook in	crochet hook.
crochet	top of first dc made,	
inc increase	insert hook back in	**Size**
patt pattern	dropped loop (2 loops	One size.
rep repeat	on hook), yo and pull	
RS right side	yarn through	**Finished**
sc single crochet	**Cuff Popcorn**	**measurement**
sc2tog single crochet	(popcorn for cuff) 4dc	Tip of finger to bottom
2 stitches together	in next sp, remove	edge of glove: 11in.
ss slip stitch	hook from loop, insert	(28cm).
sp(s) space(s)	hook in top of first dc	
st(s) stitch(es)	made, insert hook	
WS wrong side	back in dropped loop	
yo yarn over hook	(2 loops on hook), yo	
	and pull yarn through	

Left-hand Glove

Make 120ch, join with hdc in first ch.

Round 1: [2ch, skip 2 ch, 1dc in next ch] 39 times, 2ch, skip 2 ch, 1dc in first 2-ch sp. (40 sps)

Round 2: 2ch, 1dc in same ch sp as joining dc, [2ch, 1dc in next 2-ch sp] 13 times, *1ch, Popcorn in next 2-ch sp, 1ch, 1dc in next 2-ch sp, [2ch, 1dc in next 2-ch sp] twice; rep from * 3 times more, [2ch, 1dc in next 2-ch sp] 10 times.

Round 3: [2ch, 1dc in next 2-ch sp] 14 times, *2ch, 1dc in 1-ch sp (before Popcorn), 2ch, 1dc in 1-ch sp (after Popcorn), [2ch, 1dc in next 2-ch sp] twice; rep from * 3 times more, [2ch, 1dc in next 2-ch sp] 10 times.

Round 4: [2ch, 1dc in next 2-ch sp] 16 times, *1ch, Popcorn in next 2-ch sp, 1ch, 1dc in next 2-ch sp, [2ch, 1dc in next 2-ch sp] twice; rep from * 2 more times, [2ch, 1dc in next 2-ch sp] 12 times.

Round 5: [2ch, 1dc in next 2-ch sp] 16 times, *2ch, 1dc in 1-ch sp (before Popcorn), 2ch, 1dc in 1-ch sp (after Popcorn), [2ch, 1dc in next 2-ch sp] twice; rep from * 2 more times, [2ch, 1dc in next 2-ch sp] 12 times.

Round 6: [2ch, 1dc in next 2-ch sp] 14 times, *1ch, Popcorn in next 2-ch sp, 1ch, 1dc in next 2-ch sp, [2ch, 1dc in next 2-ch sp] twice; rep from * 3 more times, [2ch, 1dc in next 2-ch sp] 10 times.

Tips

These gloves are made in a spiral so each round is continuous, therefore it's very important to use a stitch marker to indicate the beginning of each round. The stitch marker is placed around the last stem at the end of each round. It's easy to make an error when working with fine crochet, so it's advisable to use a new stitch marker on each round and leave the old one in, so that you can count back your rounds more easily.

It's essential that you count the spaces on the first round, to ensure that you have the correct number to be able to continue.

Round 7: [2ch, 1dc in next 2-ch sp] 14 times, *2ch, 1dc in 1-ch sp (before Popcorn), 2ch, 1dc in 1-ch sp (after Popcorn), [2ch, 1dc in next 2-ch sp] twice; rep from * 3 more times, [2ch, 1dc in next 2-ch sp] 10 times.

Round 8 (inc round): [2ch, 1dc in next 2-ch sp] twice, 2ch, 1dc, 1ch, 1dc in next 2-ch sp, [2ch, 1dc in next 2-ch sp] 5 times, 2ch, 1dc, 1ch, 1dc in next 2-ch sp, [2ch, 1dc in next 2-ch sp] 7 times, *1ch, Popcorn in next 2-ch sp, 1ch, 1dc in next 2-ch sp, [2ch, 1dc in next 2-ch sp] twice; rep from * twice, [2ch, 1dc in next 2-ch sp] 12 times.

Round 9: [2ch, 1dc in next 2-ch sp] 3 times, 2ch, 1dc in 1-ch sp, [2ch, 1dc in next 2-ch sp] 6 times, 2ch, 1dc in next 1-ch sp, [2ch, 1dc in next 2-ch sp] 7 times, *2ch, 1dc in 1-ch sp (before Popcorn), 2ch, 1dc in 1-ch sp (after Popcorn), [2ch, 1dc in next 2-ch sp] twice; rep from * twice, [2ch, 1dc in next 2-ch sp] 12 times.

Round 10: [2ch, 1dc in next 2-ch sp] 16 times, *1ch, Popcorn in next 2-ch sp, 1ch, 1dc in next 2-ch sp, [2ch, 1dc in next 2-ch sp] twice; rep from * 3 more times, [2ch, 1dc in next 2-ch sp] 10 times.

Round 11: [2ch, 1dc in next 2-ch sp] 3 times, 2ch, 1dc, 1ch, 1dc in next 2-ch sp, [2ch, 1dc in next 2-ch sp] 7 times, 2ch, 1dc, 1ch, 1dc in next 2-ch sp, [2ch, 1dc in next 2-ch sp] 4 times, *2ch, 1dc in 1-ch sp (before Popcorn), 2ch, 1dc in 1-ch sp (after Popcorn), [2ch, 1dc in next 2-ch sp] twice; rep from * 3 more times, [2ch, 1dc in next 2-ch sp] 10 times.

Round 12: [2ch, 1dc in next 2-ch sp] 4 times, 2ch, 1dc in 1-ch sp, [2ch, 1dc in next 2-ch sp] 8 times, 2ch, 1dc in 1-ch sp, [2ch, 1dc in next 2-ch sp] 6 times, *1ch, Popcorn in next 2-ch sp, 1ch, 1dc in next 2-ch sp, [2ch, 1dc in next 2-ch sp] twice; rep from * twice more, [2ch, 1dc in next 2-ch sp] 12 times.

Round 13: [2ch, 1dc in next 2-ch sp] 20 times, *2ch, 1dc in 1-ch sp (before Popcorn), 2ch, 1dc in 1-ch sp (after Popcorn), [2ch, 1dc in next 2-ch sp] twice; rep from * twice more, [2ch, 1dc in next 2-ch sp] 12 times.

Round 14: [2ch, 1dc in next 2-ch sp] 3 times, 2ch, 1dc, 1ch, 1dc in next 2-ch sp, [2ch, 1dc in next 2-ch sp] 10 times, 2ch, 1dc, 1ch, 1dc in next 2-ch sp, [2ch, 1dc in next 2-ch sp] 4 times, *1ch, Popcorn in next 2-ch sp, 1ch, 1dc in next 2-ch sp, [2ch, 1dc in next 2-ch sp] twice; rep from * 3 times more, [2ch, 1dc in next 2-ch sp] 10 times.

Round 15: [2ch, 1dc in next 2-ch sp] 4 times, 2ch, 1dc in 1-ch sp, [2ch, 1dc in next 2-ch sp] 9 times, 2ch, 1dc in 1-ch sp, [2ch, 1dc in next 2-ch sp] 4 times, *2ch, 1dc in 1-ch sp (before Popcorn), 2ch, 1dc in 1-ch sp (after Popcorn), [2ch, 1dc in next 2-ch sp] twice; rep from * 3 more times, [2ch, 1dc in next 2-ch sp] 10 times.

Round 16: [2ch, 1dc in next 2-ch sp] 22 times, *1ch, Popcorn in next 2-ch sp, 1ch, 1dc in next 2-ch sp, [2ch, 1dc in next 2-ch sp] twice; rep from * twice more, [2ch, 1dc in next 2-ch sp] 12 times.

Round 17: [2ch, 1dc in next 2-ch sp] 4 times, 2ch, 1dc, 1ch, 1dc in next 2-ch sp, [2ch, 1dc in next 2-ch sp] 12 times, 5ch, 1dc in 1-ch sp just made, begin thumb.

Make thumb:

Round 1: [2ch, 1dc in next 2-ch sp] 12 times, 2ch, 1dc in 3rd ch of 5-ch, 2ch, 1dc in next 2-ch sp.

Round 2: [2ch, 1dc in next 2-ch sp] 12 times.

Rep Round 2 another 8 times or to length required.

Complete thumb:

Next round: *1ch, 1dc in next 2-ch sp; rep from * to end of round.

Next round: 1sc in each ch sp to end of round.

Next round: 1sc in each sc to end of round.

Next round: Sc2tog to end of round.

Fasten off, leaving sufficient thread to pull up opening and sew in end.

Cont Round 17 of hand as follows:

Join yarn in top of last dc of Round 17 (before 5-ch), [2ch, 1dc in next 2-ch sp] 5 times, *2ch, 1dc in 1-ch sp (before Popcorn), 2ch, 1dc in 1-ch sp (after Popcorn), [2ch, 1dc in next 2-ch sp] twice; rep from * twice more, [2ch, 1dc in next 2-ch sp] 12 times.

Round 18: [2ch, 1dc in next 2-ch sp] 5 times, [2ch, 1dc in next ch sp at base of thumb] 3 times, [2ch, 1dc in next 2-ch sp] 5 times, *1ch, Popcorn in next 2-ch sp, 1ch, 1dc in next 2-ch sp, [2ch, 1dc in next 2-ch sp] twice; rep from * 3 more times, [2ch, 1dc in next 2-ch sp] 9 times.

Cont working in patt for 9 more rounds, marking last dc with stitch marker.

Next round: [2ch, 1dc in next 2-ch sp] 15 times, 5ch, count back 12 sps and work 1dc in 12th sp.

Make first finger:

Round 1: [2ch, 1dc in next 2-ch sp] 11 times, 2ch, 1dc in 3rd of 5-ch, 2ch, 1dc in next 2-ch sp.

Cont working rounds of sps until 14 rounds in all have been worked (or length required).

Complete as for thumb.

Make second finger:

Join yarn in last dc of hand (before 5-ch for base of first finger).

Round 1: [2ch, 1dc in next 2-ch sp] 5 times, 1dc in 2-ch sp before dc with stitch marker, [2ch, 1dc in next 2-ch sp] 4 times, 2ch, 1dc over dc at base of first finger, 2ch, 1dc over ch at base of finger, 2ch, skip 1dc, 1dc over ch at base of finger, [2ch, 1dc in next 2-ch sp] 5 times, 2ch, 1dc in 3rd of 5-ch, 2ch, 1dc in next 2-ch sp.

Cont working rounds of sps until 16 rounds in all have been worked (or length required).

Complete as for thumb.

Make third finger:

Join yarn in last dc before 5-ch at base of previous finger.

Round 1: [2ch, 1dc in next 2-ch sp] 4 times, 5ch, count back 5 sps from stitch marker and work 1dc in 5th sp, [2ch, 1dc in next 2-ch sp] 4 times, cont as for previous finger but working 14 rounds instead of 16 (or length required).

Complete as for thumb.
Make fourth finger:
Join thread in last dc before 5-ch at base of previous finger and cont to work rounds of sps until 11 rounds in all have been worked (or length required).
Complete as for thumb.

Cuff

Join piece of elastic to fit wrist. Join yarn to foundation ch.
Round 1: Working over elastic, 2sc in each 2-ch sp to end, join with ss in first sc.
Round 2: 5ch, skip 1 sc, 1dc in next sc, *2ch, skip 1 sc, 1dc in next sc; rep from * ending with 2ch, join with ss in 3rd of 5-ch.
Round 3: Ss in first ch sp, 3ch, 4dc in same sp, Cuff Popcorn, *2ch, 1dc in next 2-ch sp, 2ch, Cuff Popcorn in next ch sp; rep from * omitting Cuff Popcorn at end of last rep, join with ss in top of first Cuff Popcorn.
Round 4: Ss in next sp, 5ch, 1dc in next sp, *2ch, 1dc in next 2-ch sp; rep from * ending with 2ch, join with ss in 3rd of 5-ch.
Rep Rounds 3 and 4 twice more.
Round 9: Ss in first sp, 3ch, Cuff Popcorn, *2ch, Cuff Popcorn in next ch sp; rep from * ending with 2ch, join with ss in top of first Cuff Popcorn.
Round 10: Ss in first ch sp, 3ch, Cuff Popcorn, *5ch, 1sc in 4th ch from hook, Cuff Popcorn in next 2-ch sp; rep from * ending with 5ch, 1sc in 4th ch from hook, join with ss in top of first Cuff Popcorn.
Fasten off.

Right-hand Glove

Work as left-hand glove, but making increases for thumb after Popcorn sts instead of before Popcorn sts.

Finishing

Sew in ends.

IF YOU WANT TO MAKE SOMETHING A LITTLE DIFFERENT, TRY THESE SOCKS. THEY ARE A LOT OF FUN AND LOOK VERY COOL WITH SHORTS OR A SKIRT.

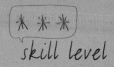

*** skill level

LONG SOCKS

MATERIALS
50% merino wool/50% cotton mix sport (4-ply) yarn, such as Rowan Wool Cotton 4-Ply

» 3 x 1¾oz (50g) balls—approx 591yd (540m)—of gray

20in. (50cm) purple ribbon

US size E/4 (3.5mm) and US size D/3 (3mm) crochet hooks

Abbreviations
ch chain
cont continue
dc double crochet
foll following
rep repeat
sc single crochet
ss slip stitch
st(s) stitch(es)
tr treble

Special abbreviation
DV-st (double V stitch)
[2dc, 1ch, 2dc]

Gauge
20 dc over 4in. (10cm) using US size E/4 (3.5mm) hook.

Size
One size.

Finished measurement
9in. (22.5cm) foot length;
16¼in. (41cm) leg length.

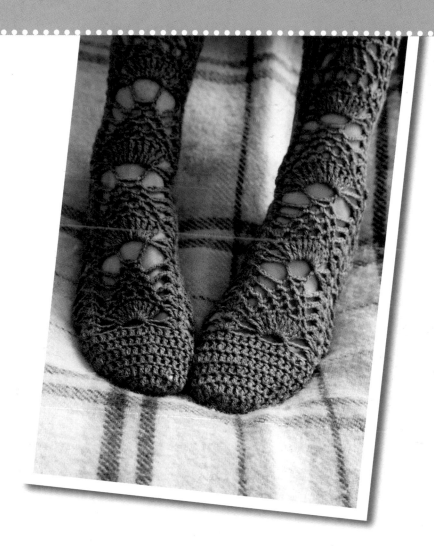

Sock

Using E/4 (3.5mm) hook, make 6ch, join with ss in first ch to form a ring.

Round 1: 3ch, 11dc in ring, join with ss in top of 3 ch.

Round 2: 3ch, 1dc in st at base of ch, [1dc in next st, 2dc in foll st] to last st, 1dc in last st, join with ss in top of 3-ch. (18 sts)

Round 3: Rep Round 2. (27 sts)

Round 4: 3ch, skip st at base of ch, 1dc in each st to end, join with ss in top of 3-ch.

Round 5: 3ch, skip st at base of ch, 1dc in next st, [2dc in next st, 1dc in each of next 2 sts] to last st, 2dc in last st, join with ss in top of 3-ch. (36 sts)

Rounds 6–7: As Round 4.

Begin Pineapple Lace st:

Round 1: 3ch, 1dc in st at base of ch, *3ch, skip next 3 dc, 1sc in next st, 5ch, skip next 3 dc, 1sc in next st, 3ch, skip 3 dc, DV-st in next st; rep from * to end omitting DV-st at end of last rep, 2dc, 1ch in same st as first dc, join with ss in top of first 3-ch.

Round 2: Ss back in last 1-ch sp of last round, 3ch, 1dc in same place, *skip next ch sp, 11tr in 5-ch sp, skip next ch sp, DV-st in 1-ch sp at center of DV-st; rep from * to end omitting DV-st at end of last rep, 2dc, 1ch in last 1-ch sp, join with ss in top of first 3-ch.

Round 3: Ss back in last 1-ch sp of last round, 3ch, 1dc in same place, *2ch, 1sc in first tr, [3ch, skip 1 tr, 1sc in next tr] 5 times, 2ch, DV-st in 1-ch sp at center of DV-st; rep from * to end omitting DV-st at end of last rep, 2dc, 1ch in last 1-ch sp, join with ss in top of first 3-ch.

Round 4: Ss back in last 1-ch sp of last round, 3ch, 1dc in same place, *skip 2-ch sp, [3ch, 1sc in next 3-ch sp] 5 times, 3ch, DV-st in 1-ch sp at center of DV-st; rep from * to end omitting DV-st at end of last rep, 2dc, 1ch in last 1-ch sp, join with ss in top of first 3-ch.

Round 5: Ss back in last 1-ch sp of last round, 3ch, 1dc in same place, *4ch, skip next 3-ch sp, 1sc in next 3-ch sp, [3ch, 1sc in next 3-ch sp] 3 times, 4ch, DV-st in 1-ch sp at center of DV-st; rep from * to end omitting DV-st at end of last rep, 2dc, 1ch in last 1-ch sp, join with ss in top of first 3-ch.

Round 6: Ss back in last 1-ch sp of last round, 3ch, 1dc in same place, *5ch, skip 4-ch sp, 1sc in 3-ch sp, [3ch, 1sc in next 3-ch sp] twice, 5ch, DV-st in 1-ch sp at center of DV-st; rep from * to end omitting DV-st at end of last rep, 2dc, 1ch in last 1-ch sp, join with ss in top of first 3-ch.

Round 7: Ss back in last 1-ch sp of last round, 3ch, 1dc in same place, *7ch, skip 5-ch sp, 1sc in 3-ch sp, 3ch, 1sc in next 3-ch sp, 7ch, DV-st in 1-ch sp at center of DV-st; rep from * to end omitting DV-st at end of last rep, 2dc, 1ch in last 1-ch sp, join with ss in top of first 3-ch.

Round 8: Ss back in last 1-ch sp of last round, 3ch, 1dc in same place, *3ch, 1sc in 7-ch sp, 5ch, skip 3-ch sp, 1sc in next 7-ch sp, 3ch, DV-st in 1-ch sp at center of DV-st; rep from * to end omitting DV-st at end of last rep, 2dc, 1ch in last 1-ch sp, join with ss in top of first 3-ch.

Rep Rounds 2–7 once more.

Fasten off.

Make heel:

Rejoin yarn to center of arch of next pineapple.

Row 1: 1ch, 3sc in 3-ch sp, [4sc, 4dc] in next 7-ch sp, 1dc in each of next 2 dc, 1dc in ch sp, 1dc in each of next 2 dc, [4dc, 4sc] in next 7-ch sp, 3sc in 3-ch sp, turn. (27 sts)

Row 2: 1ch, 1sc in each sc, 1dc in each dc, 1sc in each sc to end, 1sc in 7-ch loop of previous row, turn.

Rep last row 5 times more. (33 sts)

Make leg:

Round 1: Ss in top of 1-ch sp at center of next DV-st, work as for Round 8 of foot until heel is reached, 3ch, 1sc in 5th sc, 5ch, 1sc in 5th dc, 2ch, skip 1 dc, DV-st in next dc, 2ch, skip 1 dc, 1sc in next dc, 5ch, 1sc in 5th sc, 3ch, 2dc in center of DV-st, 1ch, join with ss in top of 3-ch.

Round 2: Change to D/3 (3mm) hook and work as Pineapple Lace st Rounds 2–8, then work Rounds 2 and 3 again.

Next round: Change to E/4 (3.5mm) hook, 5ch, *skip 2-ch sp, 1dc in first 3-ch sp, [2ch, 1dc in next 3-ch sp] 4 times, 2ch, 1dc in 1-ch sp at center of DV-st, 2ch; rep from * to end omitting dc at end of last rep, join with ss in 3rd of 5-ch. (54 sts)

Begin Spider st:

Round 1: 5ch, 1dc in st at base of ch, *2ch, 1dc in next ch sp, 4ch, 1tr in each of next 4 ch sps, 4ch, 1dc in next ch sp, 2ch, [1dc, 2ch 1dc] in next dc; rep from * to end omitting instructions in square brackets at end of last rep, join with ss in 3rd of 5-ch.

Round 2: 5ch, 1dc in next dc, *2ch, 1dc in next dc, 4ch, 1sc in each tr, 4ch, 1dc in next dc, [2ch, 1dc in next dc] twice; rep from * once, 2ch, 1dc in next dc, 4ch, 1sc in each tr, 4ch, 1dc in next dc, 2ch, join with ss in 3rd of 5-ch.

Round 3: 5ch, 1dc in next dc, *2ch, 1dc in next dc, 4ch, 1sc in each sc, 4ch, 1dc in next dc, [2ch, 1dc in next dc] twice; rep from * once, 2ch, 1dc in next dc, 4ch, 1sc in each sc, 4ch, 1dc in next dc, 2ch, join with ss in 3rd of 5-ch.

Round 4: Rep Round 3.

Round 5: 5ch, 1dc in next dc, *2ch, 1dc in next dc, [2ch, 1tr in next sc] 4 times, [2ch, 1dc in next dc] 3 times; rep from * once, 2ch, 1dc in next dc, [2ch, 1tr in next sc] 4 times, 2ch, 1dc in next dc, 2ch, join with ss in 3rd of 5-ch.

Round 6: 5ch, 1dc in next dc, [2ch, 1dc] in each dc or tr to end, join with ss in top of 3rd of 5-ch. (72 sts)
Fasten off.
Rejoin yarn to 4th dc back from join.

Round 7: 5ch, 1dc in next dc, *2ch, 1dc in next dc, 4ch, 1tr in each of next 4 dc, 4ch, 1dc in next dc, [2ch, 1dc in next dc] twice; rep from * once, 2ch, 1dc in next dc, 4ch, 1tr in each of next 4 dc, 4ch, 1dc in next dc, 2ch, join with ss in 3rd of 5-ch. (72 sts)
Work Rounds 2–6 of Spider st.
Fasten off.
Rejoin yarn to 4th dc after join. Work Round 7, then Rounds 2–6. Do not fasten off.

Next round: 5ch, 1dc in next dc, *[2dc in ch sp, 1dc in next dc] 3 times, 2ch, 1dc in next dc; rep from * to end omitting 2ch and 1dc at end or last rep, join with ss in top of 3rd of 5ch.

Next round: 3ch, 1dc in each dc and 2dc in each sp, ss to top of 3-ch.

Begin Fans:

Round 1: 3ch, 1dc in next dc, *1ch, skip 2 dc, [1dc, 3ch, 1dc] in next dc, 1ch, skip 2dc, 1dc in each of next 3 dc; rep from * to end omitting 2dc at end of last rep, join with ss in top of 3-ch.

Round 2: 4ch, *7dc in 3-ch sp, 1ch, skip 2 dc, 1dc in next dc, 1ch; rep from * to end omitting 1dc and 1ch at end of last rep, join with ss in 3rd of 4-ch.

Round 3: 6ch, 1dc in st at base of ch, *1ch, skip 2 dc, 1dc in each of next 3 dc, 1ch, skip 2 dc, [1dc, 3ch, 1dc] in next dc; rep from * to end omitting [1dc, 3ch, 1dc] at end of last rep, join with ss in 3rd of 6-ch.

Round 4: Ss in each of first 2 ch, 3ch, 3dc in sp at base of ch, *1ch, skip 2 dc, 1dc in next dc, 1ch, 7dc in 3-ch sp; rep from * ending 1ch, skip 2 dc, 1dc in next dc, 1ch, 3dc in first arch, join with ss in top of 3-ch.

Rounds 1–4 form Fan patt.
Rep Rounds 1 and 2 again.
Fasten off.
Make 2nd sock as first.

Finishing

Sew in ends.
Cut ribbon into 2 equal lengths, knot a length around center back dc on each sock on Row 1 of Fan patt, and tie in a bow.

Motif sweater

Beaded Cardigan

Circles Cardigan

Retro Chunky Jacket

Bobble sweater

Crop Top
Net Top
Tank Top
Color Block Sweater
Bobble Sweater
Fur-collared Cardigan
Retro Chunky Jacket
Peter Pan Collar Cardigan
Beaded Cardigan
Motif Sweater
Circles Cardigan
Crocodile Shawl

Crocodile Shawl

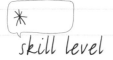
MADE WITH EASY LITTLE SQUARES THAT ARE JOINED TOGETHER, THIS FUNKY AND FASHIONABLE CROP TOP IS A GREAT BEGINNER'S PROJECT.

CROP TOP

MATERIALS

100% cotton light worsted (DK) yarn, such as Rowan Cotton Glace

>> 3 x 1¾oz (50g) balls—approx 378yd (345m)—of white (A)

>> 2 x 1¾oz (50g) balls—approx 252yd (230m)—of blue (B)

>> 1 x 1¾oz (50g) ball—approx 126yd (115m)—each of pink (C), yellow (D), pale pink (E), pale blue (F), red (G)

US size C/2 (2.5mm) crochet hook

Abbreviations		Gauge		
alt alternate		Square measures 1½in. (4cm)		
ch chain		using US size C/2 (2.5mm) hook.		
foll following				
hdc half double crochet		**Size**		
rep repeat		To fit sizes:		
RS right side			8–10	**12–14**
sc single crochet				
sc2tog single crochet		**Finished measurements**		
2 stitches together		Bust		
sc3tog single crochet		in.	31½	**33**
3 stitches together		cm	80	**84**
sp(s) space(s)		Length		
ss slip stitch		in.	15¼	**15¼**
st(s) stitch(es)		cm	38.5	**38.5**

2-color square

(Make 50 of each 2-color square [smaller size]. Make 55 of each 2-color square [larger size])

Using A, make 4ch, join with ss in first ch to form a ring.

Round 1: 3ch (counts as first hdc, 1ch), [1hdc, 1ch in ring] 7 times, join with ss in 2nd of 3-ch. (8 hdc)

Fasten off.

Round 2: Attach C, D, E, F, or G in any ch sp between hdcs, 2ch, 1hdc in same ch sp, *[1ch, 1hdc, 1ch] in next ch sp, [1hdc, 1ch, 1hdc] in next ch sp; rep from * to last ch sp, [1ch, 1hdc, 1ch] in last ch sp, join with ss in top of 2-ch.

Fasten off.

Round 3: Attach A in ch sp between any 2-hdc group, 2ch, [1sc, 1ch, 2sc] in same ch sp, [1ch, 1sc] in each of next two ch sps, 1ch, *[2sc, 1ch, 2sc, 1ch] in ch sp of next 2-hdc group, [1sc, 1ch] in each of next two ch sps; rep from * to end, join with ss in top of 2-ch.

Fasten off.

1-color square

(Make 50 of each 1-color square [smaller size]. Make 55 of each 1-color square [larger size])

Using A or B, make 4ch, join with ss in first ch to form a ring.

Round 1: 3ch (counts as first hdc, 1ch), [1hdc, 1ch in ring] 7 times, join with ss in 2nd of 3-ch. (8 hdc)

Round 2: Ss in next ch sp, 2ch, 1hdc in same ch sp, *[1ch, 1hdc, 1ch] in next ch sp, [1hdc, 1ch, 1hdc] in next ch sp; rep from * to last ch sp, [1ch, 1hdc, 1ch] in last ch sp, join with ss in top of 2-ch.

Round 3: Ss in next ch sp (between 2 ch and 1hdc from Round 2), 2ch, [1sc, 1ch, 2sc] in same ch sp, [1ch, 1sc] in each of next two ch sps, 1ch, *[2sc, 1ch, 2sc, 1ch] in ch sp of next 2-hdc group, [1sc, 1ch] in each of next two ch sps; rep from * to end, join with ss in top of 2-ch.

Fasten off.

Top

Arrange squares in 5 rows of 20 (for larger size, 5 x 22 squares) in the foll sequence:

Rows 1, 3, and 5—Alt 1 x A 1-color square and 1 x 2-color square.

Rows 2 and 4—Alt 1 x 2-color square and 1 x B 1-color square.

Join squares and rows in a panel using sc seam, and then join short ends of panel to make circular top.

Bottom edging:

Round 1: With RS facing, attach A in back seam at bottom edge, 1ch, work sc evenly around edge to end, join with ss in first sc.

Round 2: *3ch, 1sc in first ch, 1sc at base of 3-ch, skip 1 st, sc2tog, 1sc in each of next 3 sts; rep from * to end, join with ss in first sc.

Fasten off.

Top edging:

Round 1: With RS facing, attach A in back seam at top edge, 1ch, work sc evenly around edge, join with ss in first sc.

Fasten off.

Straps

(make 2)

Using B, make 3ch.

Row 1: 1sc in 2nd ch from hook, 2sc in next ch. (3 sts)

Row 2: 1ch, skip first st, 1sc in each of next 2 sts, 1sc in 1-ch from previous row. (3 sts)

Row 3: 1ch, skip first st, 2sc in next st, 1sc in next st, 2sc in 1-ch from previous row. (5 sts)

Row 4: 1ch, skip first st, 2sc in next st, 1sc in each st to end, 2sc in 1-ch from previous row. (7 sts)

Row 5: 1ch, skip first st, 1sc in each st to end, 1sc in 1-ch from previous row. (7 sts)

Rep Row 5 until work measures 15in. (38cm).

Next row: 1ch, skip first st, sc2tog, 1sc in each st to last st, sc2tog over last st and 1-ch from previous row. (5 sts)

Next row: 1ch, skip first st, sc2tog, 1sc in next st, sc2tog over last st and 1-ch from previous row. (3 sts)

Next row: 1ch, skip first st, sc2tog, 1sc in 1-ch from previous row. (3 sts)

Next row: Sc3tog.

Fasten off.

Strap edging:

With RS facing, join A in any st on long edge.

Work sc edging evenly all around strap, making 2sc in each end stitch.

Fasten off.

Crochet Buttons

(make 2)

Using A, and leaving a tail approx 15cm (6in) long, make 2ch, 5sc in 2nd ch from hook, join with ss in first ch.

Round 1: 1ch, 1sc in next st, 2sc in each of foll sts to end, join with ss in first ch.

Round 2: 1ch, 1sc in each st, join with ss in first ch.

Round 3: Sc2tog around.

Fasten off.

Turn inside out. Thread a wool/tapestry needle with yarn end, scrunch up starting tail, and stuff in center of button. Weave needle in and out around edge and pull tight to close.

Sew to secure.

Finishing

Attach straps to crop top from front to back. Sew a button to the end of each front strap for decoration.

Sew in ends.

THIS IS AN EASY TOP TO WEAR, MADE
USING AN UNCOMPLICATED STITCH AND
LIGHT AND COOL 4-PLY COTTON.

NET TOP

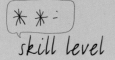

skill level

MATERIALS
100% cotton 4-ply crochet thread, such as DMC Natura
Just Cotton
>> 7 x 1¾ oz (50g) balls—approx 1187yd (1085m)—of cream

US size G/6 (4mm) and US size D/3 (3mm) crochet hooks

Abbreviations
beg beginning
ch chain
cont continue
patt pattern
rep repeat
RS right side
sc single crochet
sc2tog single crochet 2 stitches
   together
ss slip stitch
st(s) stitch(es)
tr treble
tr2tog treble 2 stitches
   together

Gauge
18 sts measure 4in. (10cm) and
12 rows measure 5in. (12.5cm)
working pattern using US size D/3
(3mm) hook.

Size
To fit sizes:

	8–10	12–14

Finished measurements
Bust

in.	35	39¼
cm	89	100

Sleeve seam

in.	7¾	7¾
cm	20	20

Length

in.	22	22¾
cm	56	58

Back
Using G/6 (4mm) hook, make 81:**91**ch.
Change to D/3 (3mm) hook.
Row 1 (RS): 1sc in second ch from hook, 1sc in each ch to end.
(80:**90** sts)
Row 2: 4ch, skip first st, 1tr in each st to end. (80:**90** sts)
Row 3: 4ch, skip first st, 1tr in each st to end, 1tr in top of 4-ch.
Row 4: 1ch, skip first st, 1sc in each st to end, 1sc in top of 4-ch.
Row 5: 1ch, skip first st, 1sc in each st to end, 1sc in 1-ch.
Row 6: 4ch, skip first st, 1tr in each st to end, 1tr in 1-ch.
Rep Rows 3–6 until work measures approx 11¾in. (30cm) ending on
a Row 3.
Do not fasten off. Take hook out of loop and drop loop, leaving loop to
be picked up later.
Sleeves:
Join another ball of yarn to top of 4-ch at beg of last row, make 34ch for
right sleeve.
Fasten off.
Next row: Pick up dropped loop and make 35ch for left sleeve, 1sc in
2nd ch from hook, 1sc in each ch, 1sc in each st across back, 1sc in
each of the 34 ch of right sleeve. (148:**158** sts)
Cont in Patt until work measures 20½:**21¼**in. (52:**54**cm) from bottom of
back, ending on a Row 3.

Front

Work as back until front is 10 rows less than back from top edge, ending with a Row 3.

Neck shaping side 1:

Row 1: 1ch, skip 1 st, 1sc in each of next 63:**68** sts, sc2tog, turn. (63:**68** sts)

Row 2: 1ch, skip first st, sc2tog, 1sc in each st to end, 1sc in 1-ch. (62:**67** sts)

Row 3: 4ch, skip first st, 1tr in each st to last st, tr2tog over last st and 1-ch. (61:**66** sts)

Row 4: 4ch, skip first st, tr2tog, 1tr in each st to end, 1tr in top of 4-ch. (60:**65** sts)

Rep Rows 1–4 twice more, then Rows 1 and 2 again.

Neck shaping side 2:

Work from where complete width of front was last worked.

With WS facing, skip 20 sts, rejoin yarn in next st.

Row 1: 1ch, skip first st, sc2tog, 1sc in each st to end, 1sc in top of 4-ch. (63:**68** sts)

Row 2: 1ch, skip first st, 1sc in each st to last st, sc2tog over last st and 1-ch. (62:**67** sts)

Row 3: 4ch, skip first st, tr2tog, 1tr in each st to end, 1tr in 1-ch. (61:**66** sts)

Row 4: 4ch, skip first st, 1tr in each st to last st, tr2tog over last st and 4-ch. (60:**65** sts)

Rep Rows 1–4 once more, then Rows 1 and 2 again.

Fasten off.

With RS together, pin shoulder sides and sleeve seams. Sew seams.

Neck Edging

Row 1: With RS facing and using D/3 (3mm) hook, join yarn at right back shoulder seam, 1ch, 1sc in each st across back neck edge, work sc evenly down left front neck to center 20 sts, work 1sc in each of center 20 sts, 1sc in each st up right front neck, join with ss in first sc.

Row 2 (picot row): Still with RS facing, *3ch, 1sc in first of 3-ch, 1sc in each of next 2 sts; rep from * to end, ss in first sc.

Fasten off.

Shape back neck:

Next row: 1ch, skip first st, 1sc in each of next 50:**55** sts, sc2tog, 1sc in each of next 44 sts, sc2tog, 1sc in each st to end, 1sc in top of 4-ch.

Next row: 1ch, skip first st, 1sc in each of next 49:**54** sts, sc2tog, 1sc in each of next 44 sts, sc2tog, 1sc in each st to end, 1sc in 1-ch.

Fasten off.

Sleeve Edging

Row 1: With RS facing and using D/3 (3mm) hook, join yarn in sleeve seam, 1ch, work 1sc in each sc row end, 1sc in between 2-tr row ends and 2sc in each tr row end, join with ss in first sc.

Row 2 (picot row): Still with RS facing, *3ch, 1sc in first of 3-ch, 1sc in each of next 2 sts; rep from * to end, join with ss in first sc. Fasten off.

Bottom Edging

Using G/6 (4mm) hook and with RS facing, join yarn in a side seam.

Round 1: 1ch, 1sc in each ch around bottom edge, join with ss in first sc.

Rounds 2–3: 1ch, 1sc in each st to end, join with ss in first sc.

Round 3 (picot row): *3ch, 1sc in first of 3-ch, 1sc in each of next 2 sts; rep from * to end, join with ss in first sc.
Fasten off.

Finishing

Sew in ends.

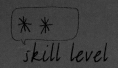
A REALLY USEFUL LITTLE TOP MADE USING A
SIMPLE TWEED STITCH, WHICH GIVES THE LOOK OF
FAIR ISLE WHEN WORKING CROCHET.

TANK TOP

MATERIALS
55% merino/33% microfiber/12% cashmere light worsted (DK) yarn,
such as Debbie Bliss Cashmerino DK
>> 2 x 1¾oz (50g) balls—approx 240yd (220m)—of black (A)

50% baby alpaca/50% merino light worsted (DK) yarn, such as
Rooster Almerino DK
>> 2 x 1¾oz (50g) balls—approx 248yd (225m)—each of off-white
(B), orange (C)

US size G/6 (4mm) crochet hook

Abbreviations
alt alternate
ch chain
cont continue
dc double crochet
hdc half double crochet
patt pattern
rem remaining
rep repeat
RS right side
sc single crochet
sc2tog single crochet
    2 stitches together
sp space
ss slip stitch
st(s) stitch(es)

Special abbreviations
fpdc (front post double) work
dc around stalk of st in previous
round from front of work

bpdc (back post double) work
dc around stalk of st in previous
round from back of work

Gauge
22 sts x 21 rows over 4in.
(10cm) square working
tweed st using US size G/6
(4mm) hook.

Size
To fit sizes:

	8	**10**	12	**14**

Finished measurements
Bust

in	32½	**34½**	36½	**33½**
cm	81	**86**	91	96

Length to shoulder

in.	20	**20**	20	20
cm	50	**50**	50	50

Back

Using A, make 79:**83**:89:**93**ch.

Row 1: Skip 2ch, 1hdc in each ch to end. (78:**82**:88:**92** sts)

Row 2: 2ch, skip first st, *1fpdc around stalk of next st, 1bpdc around stalk of next st; rep from * to last sp, 1hdc in top of 2-ch.

Row 3: 2ch, skip first st, *1bpdc around stalk of next st, 1fpdc around stalk of next st; rep from * to last sp, 1hdc in top of 2-ch.

Row 4: 1ch, 1sc in first st. *1ch, skip 1 st, 1sc in next st; rep from * to last st, 1sc in top of ch.

Do not fasten off, attach B.

Row 5: 1ch, 1sc in first st, *1ch, skip 1 st, 1sc in next ch sp; rep from * to last st, 1sc in last st.

Do not fasten off, attach C.

Row 6: Rep Row 5.

Cont to change color in this sequence, rep Row 5 until work measures 12in. (30cm).

Fasten off.

Shape armholes:

Skip first 6 sts, join yarn in next ch sp, 1ch, 1sc in same ch sp, cont in tweed st to last 7 sts, 1sc in next sc, turn. (66:**70**:76:**80** sts)*

Cont even in tweed st on these sts until back measures 20in. (50cm).

Fasten off.

Front

Work as back to *.

Divide for neck:

Patt across first 33:**35**:38:**40** sts, turn. Work on this set of sts first.

Dec 1 st at neck edge on next and every alt row until 16:**18**:20:**22** sts rem.

Cont even until front measures same as the back.

Fasten off.

Work other side of neck to match.

Fasten off.

Sew up all seams.

Armhole edging

Join A to armhole at underarm seam, 1ch, 76sc evenly around armhole, join with ss in first sc.

Work another round of sc.

Fasten off.

Neck edging

Join A to neck at left shoulder seam, 1ch, 30sc evenly down left front neck, 1sc in center, 30sc up right front neck, 27:**27**:29:**29**sc across back neck, join with ss in first sc. (88:**88**:90:**90** sc)

Work another round of sc, working sc2tog at either side of center st.

Fasten off.

For Round Neck

With RS facing and starting at left-hand side shoulder seam, attach C. 1ch, work sc edging evenly down left side to point of V, sc2tog twice, work sc edging evenly up right side to shoulder seam, along back, join with ss in first sc.

Fasten off.

Finishing

Sew in ends.

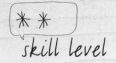
BLOCK COLORS MAKE A PLAIN SWEATER INTO AN EFFECTIVE FASHION STATEMENT. IF YOU PREFER MORE SUBTLE TONES, JUST USE PALER SHADES.

COLOR BLOCK SWEATER

MATERIALS

50% baby alpaca/50% merino mix light worsted (DK) yarn, such as Rooster Almerino DK

>> 3:**3**:3 x 1¾oz (50g) balls—approx 372:**372**:372yd (337.5:**337.5**:337.5m)— each of blue (A), bright pink (B)

>> 3:**3**:4 x 1¾oz (50g) balls—approx 372:**372**:496yd (337.5:**337.5**:450m)— of off-white (C)

>> 3:**4**:4 x 1¾oz (50g) balls—approx 372:**496**:496yd (337.5:**450**:450m)— of yellow (D)

>> 2:**2**:3 x 1¾oz (50g) balls—approx 248:**248**:372yd (225:**225**:337.5m)— of red (E)

US size D/3 (3mm), US size E/4 (3.5mm), and US size G/6 (4mm) crochet hooks

Abbreviations

alt alternate

beg beginning

ch chain

dc double crochet

dc2tog double crochet 2 stitches together

foll following

inc increase

patt pattern

rep repeat

RS right side

sc single crochet

sc3tog single crochet 3 stitches together

ss slip stitch

st(s) stitch(es)

WS wrong side

yo yarn over hook

Special Abbreviations

2Cdc (2 crossed double stitches) skip next st, 1dc in next st, 1dc in skipped st working over first dc

Gauge

18 sts x 14 rows over 4in. (10cm) square working main patt using US size E/4 (3.5mm) hook.

Size

To fit sizes:

	8–10	**10–12**	12–14

Finished measurements

Bust			
in.	39¾	**41**	42¾
cm	100	**104**	108.5
Length			
in.	22½	**22½**	22½
cm	57	**57**	57
Sleeve length			
in.	16	**16**	16
cm	41	**41**	41

Tips

To work the second of the crossed doubles, insert the hook in the skipped stitch, yo, bring loop through, and then complete the stitch normally. The second stitch crosses over the first stitch made, and sandwiches it.

When changing colors, just before you work the last step of the last stitch using the old yarn, drop the old yarn and pick up the new yarn, draw it through to complete the stitch: new yarn joined in.

Leave a length of the yarn before joining in a new color—this can be used to sew up side and sleeve seams.

Main Pattern

Row 1 (RS): 3ch (counts as 1dc), skip first sc, * work 2Cdc over next 2 sc; rep from * ending 1dc in last sc.

Row 2: 1ch, 1sc in first dc, 1sc in each dc to end, working last sc in top of 3-ch.

Rows 1 and 2 form patt.

Work in the foll color sequence:

Using A work 10:**10**:10 rows.

Using B work 16:**16**:16 rows.

Using C work 16:**16**:16 rows.

Using D work 16:**16**:16 rows.

Using E work 16:**16**:16 rows.

Back

Welt:

Using E/4 (3.5mm) hook and A, make 91:**95**:99ch.

Row 1 (RS): 1sc in 2nd ch from hook, 1sc in each ch to end. (90:**94**:98 sc)

Next row: 1ch, 1sc in each sc to end.

Rep last row 8 times more.

Main body:

Beg with Row 1 of Main Patt, work even for 72:**72**:72 rows.

Shape neck:

Next row: With RS facing, 3ch (counts as 1dc), skip first sc, *2Cdc over next 2 sc; rep from * 12:**13**:14 times more, 1dc in next st, turn.

Next row: 1ch, 1sc in each st to end.

With RS facing, return to last complete row worked, skip next 34:**34**:34 sts, rejoin yarn to foll st, 3ch, *2Cdc over next 2 sc; rep from * 12:**13**:14 times more, 1dc in last sc.

Next row: 1ch, 1sc in each st to end.

Fasten off.

Front

Using E/4 (3.5mm) hook and A, make 91:**95**:99ch.

Work 10 rows of sc as for back.

Beg with Row 1 of Main Patt, work even for 59 rows.

Shape right front neck:

With WS facing for next row and keeping color sequence correct, 1ch, 1sc in each of first 36:**38**:40 sts, turn.

Row 1: Ss across first 3 sts, 3ch (counts as first st), dc2tog, patt to end. (33:**35**:37 sts)

Row 2: 1ch, 1sc in each st to end.

Row 3: 3ch (counts as first st), dc2tog, 1dc in next st, patt to end.

Row 4: As Row 2.

Row 5: 3ch (counts as first st), dc2tog, patt to end.

Rep Rows 2–5 once more, then Rows 2–3 again. (28:**30**:32 sts)

Patt 3 rows even.

Fasten off.

Shape left front neck:

With WS facing, return to last complete row worked, skip next (center) 18 sts, rejoin yarn to next st, patt to end. (36:**38**:40 sts)

Complete to match first side, reversing shaping.

Fasten off.

Sleeves

(make 2)

Work inc sts as dcs until a complete 2Cdc can be worked.

Color sequence worked in main patt:

Using B, work 10:**10**:10 rows.

Using C, work 16:**16**:16 rows.

Using D, work 16:**16**:16 rows.

Using G/6 (4mm) hook and A, make 33:**33**:37ch.

Row 1 (RS): 1sc in 2nd ch from hook, 1sc in each ch to end. (32:**32**:36 sc)

Change to US size E/4 (3.5mm) hook.

Next row: 1ch, 1sc in each sc to end.

Rep last row 10 times more.

With RS facing, change to B and work 11 rows in sc.

Next row (inc): 1ch, 1sc in each of first 3:**3**:5 sc, *2sc in next sc, 1sc in each of next 4 sc; rep from * 4 times more, 2sc in foll sc, 1sc in each sc to end. (38:**38**:42 sc)

Still using B, begin color sequence and patt for sleeves, at the same time working the foll:

Work 4 rows in patt.

Next row (inc): 3ch, 1dc in same place as 3-ch, patt to last st, 2dc in last sc. (40:**40**:44 sc)

Inc 1 st each end as set by last row on foll 3:**3**:4 alt rows, then on every foll 4th row 6:**6**:6 times. (58:**58**:64 sts)

Work even for 7:**7**:5 rows.

Fasten off.

Neckband

Join shoulder seams.

Using D/3 (3mm) hook and E, start at left shoulder and work 22:**22**:22sc down left front neck, 21:**21**:21sc across front neck, 22:**22**:22sc up right front neck, 42:**42**:42 sc around back neck, join with ss in first sc, do not turn. (107:**107**:107 sc)

Round 1: 1sc in each sc around, working sc3tog in both front and back inner corners.

Round 2: 1sc in each sc.

Rep Rounds 1 and 2 once more.

Fasten off.

Finishing

Place markers along side seam edges 16:**16**:18.5cm (6½:**6½**:7½in) on either side of shoulder seams. Place center of fastened-off edge of sleeve to shoulder seam. Sew top of sleeve to body, using markers as a guideline. Sew up side and sleeve seams.

THE BOBBLES ON THIS SWEET LITTLE
SWEATER GIVE IT A GREAT TEXTURE, SO
IT'S BEST MADE IN A SOFT COLOR.

 *skill level*

BØBBLE SWEATER

MATERIALS

50% baby alpaca/50% merino mix light worsted (DK) yarn, such as Rooster Almerino DK

>> 21:**22**:24:**25**:27 x 1¾oz (50g) balls—approx 2604:**2728**:2976:**3100**:3348yd (2362.5:**2475**:2700:**2812.5**:2037.5m)—of pale blue

US size E/4 (3.5mm) and US size G/6 (4mm) crochet hooks

Size
To fit sizes:

8	**10**	12	**14**	16

Finished measurements
Bust

	8	**10**	12	**14**	16
in.	35¾	**38½**	41¼	**44**	47¼
cm	91	98	105	95	112
Length					
in.	21½	**22**	22½	**23**	23½
cm	54	55	56	57	58
Sleeve length					
in.	19	**19**	19	**19**	19
cm	47	47	47	47	47

Abbreviations
beg begin
ch chain
cont continue
dc double crochet
dec decrease
patt pattern
rep repeat
RS right side
sc single crochet
sc2tog single crochet
 2 stitches together
ss slip stitch
st(s) stitch(es)
yo yarn over hook

Special abbreviation
dc5CL (5 double cluster) leaving the last loop of each dc on hook, work 5dc in next sc, yo, draw through all loops on hook, 1ch (1 dc5CL completed)

Gauge
17 sts and 19 rows over 4in. (10cm) square working patt using US size G/6 (4mm) crochet hook.

Back

Using G/6 (4mm) hook, make 79:**85**:91:**97**:103ch.
Foundation row: 1sc in 2nd ch from hook, 1sc in each ch to end. 78:**84**:90:**96**:102 sts
Next row: 1ch, 1sc in each sc to end.
Rep last row until back measures 2¼in. (6cm).
Begin working in patt.
Row 1 (WS): 1ch, [1sc in each of next 2 sc, 1dc5CL in next sc] to end.
Row 2: 1ch, [1sc in top of dc5CL, 1sc in each of next 2 sc] to end.
Row 3: 1ch, [1dc5CL in next sc, 1sc in each of next 2 sc] to end.
Row 4: 1ch, [1sc in each of next 2 sc, 1sc in top of dc5CL] to end.
These 4 rows form patt.
Cont in patt until back measures 14¼:**14½**:14½:**14½**:15in. (36:**37**:37:**37**:38cm), ending with a patt Row 2 or 4.
Shape armholes:
Row 1: Ss across first 4 sc, 1ch, 1sc in same place as last ss, patt to last 3 sc, turn. (72:**78**:84:**90**:96 sts)
Row 2: 1ch, sc2tog, patt to last 2 sts, sc2tog.
Row 3: Patt to end.
Rep last 2 rows 2:**5**:5:**8**:8 times more. (66:**66**:72:**72**:78 sts)**
Work even until back measures 21¼:**21¾**:22:**22½**:22¾in. (54:**55**:56:**57**:58cm), ending with a patt Row 1 or Row 3.
Fasten off.

Front

Work as for back to **.

Shape neck:

Next row: 1ch, 1sc in first sc, 1sc in each of next 21:**21**:23:**23**:25 sts, turn.

Work on these sts for first side of neck.

Next row: Patt to end.

Next row: Patt to last 2 sts, sc2tog.

Rep the last 2 rows 4 times more. (17:**17**:19:**19**:21 sts)

Cont even in patt until front measures the same as back.

Fasten off.

Skip center 22:**22**:24:**24**:26 sc, rejoin yarn to foll sc, 1ch, patt to end.

Next row: Patt to end.

Next row: Sc2tog, patt to end.

Rep the last 2 rows 4 times more. (17:**17**:19:**19**:21 sts)

Cont even in patt until front measures the same as back.

Fasten off.

Sleeve

(make 2)

Using G/6 (4mm) hook, make 37:**40**:40:**43**:43ch.

Foundation row: 1sc in 2nd ch from hook, 1sc in each ch to end. (36:**39**:39:**42**:42 sts)

Next row: 1ch, 1sc in each sc to end.

Rep the last row until sleeve measures 2¼in. (6cm).

Beg working in patt.

Row 1: 1ch, [1sc in each of next 2 sc, 1dc5CL in next sc] to end.

Row 2: 1ch, [1sc in top of dc5CL, 1sc in each of next 2 sc] to end.

Row 3: 1ch, [1dc5CL in next sc, 1sc in each of next 2 sc] to end.

Row 4: 1ch, [1sc in each of next 2 sc, 1sc in top of dc5CL] to end.

These 4 rows form patt.

Inc row: 1ch, 1sc in first st, 2sc in next st, patt to last 2 sts, 2sc in next st, 1sc in last st, turn.

Work 4 rows even.

Taking inc sts into patt, rep the last 6 rows 8 times more, then work first 2 of the rows again. (56:**59**:59:**62**:62 sts)

Work even until sleeve measures 18½in. (47cm), ending with a patt Row 2 or 4.

Mark each end of last row with a colored thread.

Work 3 rows.

Shape sleeve top:

1st row: 1ch, sc2tog, patt to last 2 sts, sc2tog, turn.

2nd row: Patt to end, turn.

Rep the last 2 rows 2:**5**:5:**8**:8 times more. (50:**47**:47:**44**:44 sts)

Fasten off.

Neck Edging

Join shoulder seams.

With RS facing, keeping gauge correct and using E/4 (3.50mm) hook, attach yarn to left shoulder, 1ch, work sc all around neck edge, ss in first sc.

Round 1: 1ch, 1sc in each st to end, join with ss in first sc.

Place pin/stitch marker at 4 points around neck—1 at each shoulder seam, 1 at each side of center front neck sts.

Round 2: Dec 4 sts evenly around neck as follows: 1ch, 1sc in each st around, sc2tog at each pin marker, join with ss in first sc. (4 sts dec)

Round 3: 1ch, [1sc in each st to start of dec from previous round, sc2tog over dec] 4 times, 1sc in each st to end. (4 sts dec)

Rep Round 3.

Fasten off.

Finishing

Sew in ends. Join side and sleeve seams. Set in sleeves, sewing the ends of 3 rows above markers to sts of Row 1 of armhole shaping on back and front. Join side and sleeve seams.

FUR-COLLARED CARDIGAN  *skill level*

AN ELEGANT CARDIGAN WITH A DELICATE
OPEN STITCH DESIGN—IT MAY NOT HAVE
A REAL FUR COLLAR, BUT THE CROCHET
VERSION LOOKS JUST AS STYLISH.

MATERIALS

50% baby alpaca/50% merino mix light worsted
(DK) yarn, such as Rooster Almerino DK
>> 10:**11**:11:**12**:12 x 1¾oz (50g) balls—approx
1240:**1364**:1364:**1488**:1488yd
(1125:**1237.5**:1237.5:**1350**:13650m)—of
pale pink (A)

55% merino/33% microfiber/12% cashmere
light worsted (DK) yarn, such as Debbie Bliss
Cashmerino DK
>> 2:**2**:2:**2**:2 x 1¾oz (50g) balls—approx 240yd
(220m)—of brown (B)

US size C/2 (2.5mm), US size D/3 (3mm), and
US size E/4 (3.5mm) crochet hooks

6 pearl buttons, ½in. (10mm) in diameter

Abbreviations
alt alternate
ch chain
cont continue
dc double crochet
dc2tog double crochet
  2 stitches together
dec decrease(d)
hdc half double
  crochet
patt pattern
rep repeat
RS right side
sc single crochet
sp space
ss slip stitch
st(s) stitch(es)
tog together
WS wrong side

Special abbreviations
V-st (V stitch) [1dc, 1ch, 1dc] in 1-ch space
DV-st (Double V stitch) [2dc, 1ch, 2dc] in
1-ch space

Gauge
24 sts and 10 rows over 4in. (10cm) square
working Patt using US size E/4 (3.5mm) hook.

Size
To fit sizes:

8	10	12	14	16

Finished measurements
Bust

	8	10	12	14	16
in.	31½	**33½**	35½	**37½**	39½
cm	80	**85**	90	**95**	100

Length to shoulder

	8	10	12	14	16
in.	20½	**20½**	20½	**21¼**	22
cm	52	**52**	52	**54**	55

Sleeve length

	8	10	12	14	16
in.	18½	**18½**	18½	**18½**	18½
cm	47	**47**	47	**47**	47

Pattern

Foundation row (WS): V-st in 5th ch from hook, * skip 2 ch, V-st in next ch; rep from * to last 2ch, skip 1ch, 1dc in last ch, turn.

Row 1: 3ch, skip 2 sts, DV-st in ch sp at center of V-st, *1ch, skip next V-st, DV-st in sp at center of next V-st; rep from * leaving last loop of last dc of last DV-st on hook and work it together with 1dc in top of 3-ch.

Row 2: 3ch, V-st in each ch sp to end, finishing 1dc in top of 3-ch.

Row 3: 3ch, 1dc in first st, * 1ch, skip next V-st, DV-st in space at center of next V-st; rep from * until 1 V-st remains, 1ch, skip V-st, 2dc in top of 3-ch.

Row 4: As Row 2.

Rows 1–4 form patt; rep throughout unless instructed otherwise.

Back

Using E/4 (3.5mm) hook and A, make 97:**103**:109:**115**:121ch.

Work Foundation row of Patt. (31:**33**:35:**37**:39 V-sts)

Work Rows 1–4 of Patt, then change to D/3 (3mm) hook. Cont working in Patt until a total of 20 rows have been worked.

Change to E/4 (3.5mm) hook and work a further 13:**13**:13:**15**:15 rows, ending with a Row 4:4:4:2:2. (33:**33**:33:**35**:35 rows in total)

*Armhole shaping 1st, **2nd**, and 3rd sizes only:*

Ss across first 6 sts, 3ch, DV-st in next V-st, patt to last 8 sts, leaving last loop of last dc of last DV-st on hook and work it tog with 1dc in first dc of next V-st, turn. (12 sts dec)

*Armhole shaping **4th** and 5th sizes only:*

Ss across first 6 sts, 3ch, 1dc in next dc, 1ch, patt to last 3 V-sts, 1ch, skip next V-st, 2dc in next dc, turn. (12 sts dec)

All sizes:

Work even for a further 17:**17**:17:**17**:19 rows.

Fasten off.

Place a marker 23:**26**:29:**32**:35 sts in from armhole edge on both sides to denote shoulder.

Right Front

1st, 3rd, and 5th sizes only:

Using E/4 (3.5mm) hook and A, make 49:55:61ch.

Work Foundation row of Patt. (15:17:19 V-sts)

Work Rows 1–4 of Patt, then change to D/3 (3mm) hook.

Cont working in Patt until a total of 20 rows have been worked.

Change to E/4 (3.5mm) hook and work a further 13:13:15 rows, ending with a Row 4:4:2. (33:33:35 rows in total)

2nd and 4th sizes only:

Using E/4 (3.5mm) hook and A, make **52**:**58**ch.

Work Foundation row of Patt. (**16**:**18** sts)

Row 1: 3ch, skip 2 sts, DV-st in ch sp at center of first V-st, *1ch, skip next V-st, DV-st in sp at center of next V-st; rep from * to last V-st, 1ch, skip V-st, 2dc in top of 3-ch.

Row 2: 3ch, V-st in each sp to end, finishing 1dc in top of 3-ch.

Row 3: 3ch, 1dc in first st, * 1ch, skip next V-st, DV-st in sp at center of next V-st; rep from * leaving last loop of last dc of last DV-st on hook and work it together with 1dc in top of 3-ch.

Row 4: As Row 2.

Change to D/3 (3mm) hook and cont working in Patt until a total of 20 rows have been worked.

Change to E/4 (3.5mm) hook and work a further **13:15** rows, ending with a Row **4:2**. (**33:35** rows in total)

*Armhole shaping 1st, 3rd, and **4th** sizes only:*

Patt to last 8 sts leaving last loop of last dc of last DV-st on hook and work it together with a dc in first dc of next V-st, turn. (6 sts dec)

*Armhole shaping **2nd** and 5th sizes only:*

Patt to last 3 V-sts, 1ch, skip next V-st, 2dc in next dc, turn. (6 sts dec)

*Neck shaping 1st, **2nd**, and 3rd sizes only:*

With RS facing, ss across first 15 sts, 3ch, 1dc in same V-st center sp, 1ch, skip next V-st, DV-st in next V-st center sp, patt to end, turn.

Row 1: Patt to last 1-ch space, 1dc in last 1-ch sp, 1ch, work 1dc in same 1-ch sp as last dc tog with 1dc in top of 3-ch. (1 st dec)

Row 2: Ss in first 1-ch sp, 4ch (counts as 1dc, 1ch), 1dc in same sp, 1ch, skip next V-st, DV-st onto next V-st, patt to end. (1 st dec)

Row 3: Patt to last 4 ch, 1dc in 4-ch loop. (1 st dec)

*Neck shaping **4th** and 5th sizes only:*

With RS facing, ss across first 15 sts, 3ch, DV-st in next V-st, patt to end.

Row 1: Patt to last DV-st, 1dc in 1-ch sp, 1ch, 1dc in same 1-ch sp as last dc tog with 1dc in top of 3-ch. (1 st dec)

Row 2: Ss in 1-ch sp, 3ch, DV-st in next V-st, patt to end. (1 st dec)

Row 3: Patt to last DV-st, V-st in this center sp, 1dc in top of 3-ch, turn. (1 st dec)

All sizes:

Work even for **2:2:2:2:4** rows.

Fasten off.

Left Front

1st, 3rd, and 5th sizes only:

Work as for right front, reversing armhole and neck shapings.

*2nd and **4th** sizes only:*

Using E/4 (3.5mm) hook and A, make **52:58**ch.

Work Foundation row of Patt. (**16:18** sts)

Row 1: 3ch, 1dc in first st, * 1ch, skip next V-st, DV-st in sp at center of next V-st; rep from * leaving last loop of last dc of last DV-st on hook and work it together with 1dc in top of 3-ch.

Row 2: 3ch, V-st in each space to end, finishing 1dc in top of 3-ch.

Row 3: 3ch, skip 2 sts, DV-st in ch sp at center of V-st, *1ch, skip next V-st, DV-st in sp at center of next V-st; rep from * to last V-st, 1ch, skip V-st, 2dc in top of 3-ch.

Row 4: As Row 2.

Change to D/3 (3mm) hook and cont working in Patt until a total of 20 rows have been worked.

Change to E/4 (3.5mm) hook and work a further **13:15** rows, ending with a Row **4:2**.

Cont as for right front, reversing armhole and neck shapings.

Neck Edging

Join shoulder and side seams.

With RS facing, rejoin A to top right front neck edge.

Using D/3 (3mm) hook, 1ch, work 27:**27**:27:**27**:31sc evenly up right front neck, 32sc across back neck, and 27:**27**:27:**27**:31sc down left front neck. (86:**86**:86:**86**:94 sc)

Work 1 row sc.

Fasten off.

Body Edging

With RS facing, join A to top of left front at end of 2nd row of neck edging.

Using D/3 (3mm) hook, work 1 row of sc down left front edge, 3sc in bottom corner st, 1 row of sc along hem, 3sc in bottom right corner st, 1 row of sc up right front edge, turn.

Change to C/2 (2.5mm) hook.

Buttonhole row: 1ch, 1sc in each of first 3 sc, [3ch, skip 2sc] once (buttonhole made), work a further 5 buttonholes evenly down right front edge, placing 5th buttonhole 3¾in. (9cm) from bottom edge.

Cont working 1sc in each sc of previous row and 3sc in both lower corner sts, working along hem and up to top of left front edge, turn.

Work 1 more row of sc along both front edges and hem, working 2sc in each 3-ch space for buttonhole.

Fasten off.

Sleeves

(Make 2)

Using D/3 (3mm) hook and B, make 36:**36**:36:**36**:42ch.

Row 1: 1sc in 2nd ch from hook, 1sc in each ch to end; do not turn.

Cont with RS of cuff facing on every row.

Row 2: Working from left to right, *7ch, ss in front loop only of next sc to right; rep from * to end, working last ss in st at base of 7-ch; do not turn.

Row 3: Working from right to left, 1ch, 1sc in back loop only of each st to end; do not turn.

Rep Rows 2 and 3 once more, then Row 2 again.

Change to A.

Next row: 1ch, 1sc in first sc, 1sc in each of next 5:**5**:5:**5**:6 sc, *2sc in next sc, 1sc in each of next 5:**5**:5:**5**:6 sc; rep from * to end. (41:**41**:41:**41**:47 sc)

Change to E/4 (3.5mm) hook.

Next row (WS): 3ch (counts as first dc), skip first 2 sc, V-st in next sc, *skip 2 sc, V-st in next sc, rep from * to last 2 sc, skip 1 sc, 1dc in last sc, turn. (13:**13**:13:**13**:15 V-sts)

Next row: Working patt as set for back, work Row 1 of Patt.

Inc row: 3ch, 1dc in same place as 3ch (inc st), work Row 2 of Patt as set to end, working 2dc in top of 3-ch.

Next row: 3ch, skip first dc, 2dc in next dc, 1ch, Patt as Row 3, ending 2dc in last dc, 1dc in 3rd of 3-ch.

Inc row: 3ch, 1dc in same place as 3-ch, 1dc in next dc, Patt as Row 4, working an extra dc in last st.

Cont working 4-row Patt, inc 1 st each end of every alt row until there are 83:**83**:83:**83**:89 sts.

Work even until sleeve measures 18½in. (47cm).

Fasten off.

Collar

With RS facing, attach B to right front neck at inner edge of 3-row body edging.

Using D/3 (3mm) hook, 1ch, work 1 row of sc around neck edge to inner edge of 3-row body edging on left front, turn.

Row 1: Working from right to left: 1ch, 1sc in back loop of each sc to end, do not turn.

Row 2: Working from left to right, *7ch, ss in front loop only of next st to right; rep from * to end, working last ss in st at base of 7-ch; do not turn.

Row 3: Working from right to left, 2ch, 1hdc in back loop of each st on row below last row; do not turn.

Rep Rows 2 and 3 until collar measures 1¼in. (3cm), then inc 10 sts evenly across hdc row, working first and last inc 3 sts in from each end of collar.

Cont in Patt until collar measures 2in. (5cm), ending with a Row 2.

Fasten off.

Finishing

Sew up sleeve seams and set in sleeves.

Sew on buttons to correspond to buttonholes.

Tip

When shaping sleeves, if you cannot complete a single V stitch or Double V stitch when increasing, work in dc until you can.

A LOOSE-FITTING JACKET IN FLORET STITCH WITH A FAIRISLE-LOOK WAVE-&-CHEVRON STRIPE, DOUBLE CROCHET EDGING AND DEEP ROLLED DOUBLE COLLAR.

RETRO CHUNKY JACKET

MATERIALS

50% baby alpaca/50% merino mix worsted (Aran) yarn, such as Rooster Almerino Aran

>> 14:**15**:15 x 1¾oz (50g) balls—approx 1442:**1545**:1545yd (1316:**1410**:1410m)—of off-white (A)

>> 2:**2**:2 x 1¾oz (50g) balls—approx 206:**206**:206yd (188:**188**:188m)—of purple (B)

>> 1:**1**:1 x 1¾oz (50g) balls—approx 103:**103**:103yd (94:**94**:94m)—each of yellow (C), coral (D)

US size I/9 (5.5mm) crochet hook

5 x ⅞in. (21mm) buttons

Abbreviations

ch chain
cont continue
dc double crochet
dc3tog double crochet 3 stitches together
dec decreasing
foll follows/following
hdc half double crochet
hdc2tog half double crochet 2 stitches together
inc increase(d)
patt pattern
rep(s) repeat(s)
RS right side

sc single crochet
sc2tog single crochet 2 stitches together
sc3tog single crochet 3 stitches together
sp space
ss slip stitch
st(s) stitch(es)
tr treble crochet
tr2tog treble 2 stitches together
tr3tog treble 3 stitches together
WS wrong side

Gauge

13 sts x 11 rows measures 4in. (10cm) square working Floret Patt using US size I/9 (5.5mm) hook.
12 rows of Wave-&-Chevron Patt measure 4½in. (11.5cm) using US size I/9 (5.5mm) hook.

Size

To fit sizes:

	8–10	**10–12**	12–14

Finished measurements

Actual measurement

	8–10	**10–12**	12–14
in.	39¾	**44**	46¾
cm	101	**112**	119
To fit bust			
in.	30–32	**32–34**	34–36
cm	76–81	**81–86**	86–91
Length (excluding hemband)			
in.	24	**24**	24
cm	60	**60**	60
Sleeve length			
in.	19	**19**	19
cm	47	**47**	47

Tip

One side of the collar will have a tendency to curl under, whereas the other side may not. To correct this, block and gently roll each side under.

Floret Pattern

Row 1 (RS): 1dc in 4th ch from hook and each ch to end.
Row 2: 1ch, skip first st, *1dc in next st, ss in foll st; rep from * to end, ss in 3rd of 3-ch from previous row.
Row 3: 3ch (counts as dc), skip first st, 1dc in each st to end, 1dc in 1-ch from previous row.
Rep Rows 2–3 once more.

Wave-&-Chevron Pattern

Using first color, 1sc in 2nd ch from hook, 1sc in each ch to end.
Row 1 (RS): Change to 2nd color, 1ch (counts as first st), skip first st, *1hdc in next st, 1dc in foll st, 3tr in next st, 1dc in foll st, 1hdc in next st, 1sc in foll st; rep from * ending 1sc in last st from previous row.
Row 2: Change to 3rd color, skip first st, 1sc in each of next 3 sts, 3sc in next st (center tr from previous row), 1sc in each of next 2 sts, *sc3tog, 1sc in each of next 2 sts, 3sc in foll st, 1sc in each of next 2 sts, rep from * to last st, sc2tog over last st and 1-ch from previous row.
Row 3: Change to 4th color, skip first st, 1sc in each of next 3 sts, *3sc in foll st, 1sc in each of next 2 sts, sc3tog, 1sc in each of next 2 sts, rep from * to last 5 sts, 3sc in next st, 1sc in each of foll 2 sts, sc2tog.
Row 4: Change to 2nd color, 3ch (does not count as a st), skip first st, 1tr in next st, 1dc in foll st, *1hdc in next st, 1sc in foll st, 1hdc in next st, 1dc in foll st, tr3tog, 1dc in next st; rep from * to last 6 sts, 1hdc in next st, 1sc in foll st, 1hdc in next st, 1dc in foll st, tr2tog.
Row 5: Change to 3rd color, 1ch (counts as first st), 1sc in each st to end.
Row 6: Change to 4th color, 1ch (counts as first st), 1sc in each st to end, 1sc in 1-ch.
Rep Rows 1–6 once more.

Back

Using A, make 65:**71**:77ch. Begin working Floret Patt.
Row 1 (RS): 1dc in 4th ch from hook, 1dc in each ch to end. (63:**69**:75 sts)
Row 2: 1ch (counts as first st), skip first st, *1dc in next st, ss in foll st; rep from * to end, working last ss in top of 3-ch.
Row 3: 3ch (counts as first dc), skip first st, 1dc in each st to end, 1dc in 1-ch. Rep Rows 2–3 20 times more, then work Row 2 again. (44:**44**:44 rows)
Shape armholes:
Row 45 (RS): Ss across first 5 sts, 1ch (counts as first st), 1sc in each st to last 4 sts, turn. (55:**61**:67 sts)
Rows 46–57: Work Wave-&-Chevron Patt. (9:**10**:11 wave reps)
Do not turn after Row 57. Cont in Floret Patt.
Row 58: With RS facing, attach A, 3ch (counts as first dc), skip first st,

1dc in each st to end. (55:**61**:67 sts)
Row 59: 1ch, skip first st, *1dc in next st, ss in foll st; rep from * to end, working last ss in top of 3-ch.
Row 60: 3ch (counts as first dc), skip first st, 1dc in each st to end, 1dc in 1-ch.
Rep Rows 59–60 4 times more.
Fasten off.

Left Front

Using A, make 35:**39**:41ch. Begin working Floret Patt.
Row 1 (RS): 1dc in 4th ch from hook, 1dc in and each ch to end. (33:**37**:39 sts)
Row 2: 1ch, skip first st, *1dc in next st, ss in foll st; rep from * to end, working last ss in top of 3-ch.
Row 3: 3ch (counts as first dc), skip first st, 1dc in each st to end, 1dc in 1-ch. Rep Rows 2–3 17 times more, then work Row 2 again. (38:**38**:38 rows)
Shape neckline:
Row 39: 3ch (counts as first dc), skip first st, 1dc in each st to end, omitting 1ch. (32:**36**:38 sts)
Row 40: Skip first st, ss in next st, *1dc in next st, ss in foll st; rep from * to end, working last ss in top of 3-ch. (31:**35**:37 sts)
Row 41: 3ch (counts as first dc), skip first st, 1dc in each st to end, 1dc in last ss.
Row 42: Skip first st, *1dc in next st, ss in foll st; rep from * to end, working last ss in top of 3-ch. (30:**34**:36 sts)
Row 43: 3ch (counts as first dc), skip first st, 1dc in each st to end, 1dc in last dc.
Row 44: Skip first st, ss in next st, *1dc in next st, ss in next st; rep from * to end, working last ss in top of 3-ch. (29:**33**:35 sts)
Shape armholes and neckline:
Row 45 (RS): Ss across first 5 sts, 1ch (counts as first st), 1sc in each st to end. (25:**29**:31 sts)
1st and 3rd sizes only:
Row 46: Change to B, 1ch (does not count as a st), skip first st, *1hdc in next st, 1dc in foll st, 3tr in next st, 1dc in foll st, 1hdc in next st, 1sc in foll st; rep from * to end.
Row 47: Change to C, 1ch (does not count as a st), skip first st, 1sc in each of next 3 sts, 3sc in next st (center of 3-tr), 1sc in each of next 2 sts, *sc3tog, 1sc in each of next 2 sts, 3sc in next st, 1sc in each of next 2 sts, rep from * to last 9 sts, sc3tog, 1sc in each of next 2 sts, 3sc in next st, 1sc in foll st, sc2tog.
Row 48: Change to D, 1ch (does not count as a st), skip first st, 1sc in each of next 2 sts, *3sc in next st (center of 3-sc), 1sc in each of next 2 sts,

sc3tog, 1sc in each of next 2 sts, rep from * to last 5 sts, 3sc in next st, 1sc in each of next 2 sts, sc2tog.

Row 49: Change to B, 3ch (does not count as a st), skip first st, 1tr in next st, 1dc in foll st, *1hdc in next st, 1sc in foll st, 1hdc in next st, 1dc in foll st, tr3tog, 1dc; rep from * to last 4 sts, 1hdc, 1sc in next st, skip last 3 sts. (22:28 sts)

Row 50: Change to C, 1ch (counts as first st), skip first st, 1sc in each st to end.

Row 51: Change to D, 1ch (counts as first st), skip first st, 1sc in each st to end, 1sc in 1-ch

Row 52: Change to B, 3ch (does not count as a st), skip first st, 1dc in foll st, *1hdc in next st, 1sc in foll st, 1hdc in next st, 1dc in foll st, 3tr in next st, 1dc in foll st; rep from * ending 1hdc in next st, 1sc in 1-ch.

Row 53: Change to C, 1ch (does not count as a st), skip first st, 1sc in each of next 3 sts, 3sc in next st (center of 3-tr), 1sc in each of next 2 sts, *sc3tog, 1sc in each of next 2 sts, 3sc in foll st, 1sc in each of next 2 sts, rep from * to last 4 sts, sc3tog, 1sc in last st.

Row 54: Change to D, 1ch (does not count as a st), skip first st, 1sc in each of next 4 sts, *3sc in foll st (center of 3-sc), 1sc in each of next 2 sts, sc3tog, 1sc in each of next 2 sts, rep from * to last 5 sts, 3sc in next st, 1sc in each of next 2sc, sc2tog.

Row 55: Change to B, 3ch (does not count as a st), skip first st, 1tr in next st, 1dc in foll st, *1hdc in next st, 1sc in foll st, 1hdc in next st, 1dc in foll st, tr3tog, 1dc in next st; rep from * to last 3 sts, tr3tog. (19:25 sts)

Row 56: Change to C, 1ch (does not count as a st), 1sc in each st to end.

Row 57: Change to D, 1ch (does not count as a st), 1sc in each st to end, 1sc in 1-ch.

2nd size only:

Row 46: Change to B, 3ch (does not count as a st), skip first st, 2tr in next st, 1dc in foll st, 1hdc in next st, 1sc in foll st, *1hdc in next st, 1dc in foll st, 3tr in next st, 1dc in foll st, 1hdc in next st, 1sc in foll st; rep from * to end.

Row 47: Change to C, 1ch (does not count as a st), skip first st, 1sc in each of next 3 sts, *3sc in next st (center of 3-tr), 1sc in each of foll 2 sts, sc3tog, 1sc in each of next 2 sts; rep from * to last 2 sts, 2sc in next st, 1sc in last st.

Row 48: Change to D, 1ch (does not count as a st), skip first st, 2sc in next st, *1sc in each of next 2 sts, sc3tog, 1sc in each of next 2 sts, 3sc in next sc (center of 3-sc); rep from * to last 4 sts, 1sc in each of next 2 sts, sc2tog.

Row 49: Change to B, 3ch (does not count as a st), skip first st, 1tr in next st, *1dc in foll st, 1hdc in next st, 1sc in foll st, 1hdc in next st, 1dc in next st, tr3tog; rep from * to last 3 sts, dc3tog.

Row 50: Change to C, 1ch (counts as first st), skip first st, 1sc in each st to end. (26 sts)

Row 51: Change to D, 1ch (counts as first st), skip first st, 1sc in each st to end, 1sc in 1-ch.

Row 52: Change to B, 2ch (does not count as a st), skip first st, 1sc in next st, *1hdc in foll st, 1dc in next st, 3tr in foll st, 1dc in next st, 1hdc in foll st, 1sc in next st; rep from * to end.

Row 53: Change to C, 1ch (does not count as a st), skip first st, 1sc in each of next 3 sts, *3sc in foll st (center of 3-tr), 1sc in each of next 2 sts, sc3tog, 1sc in each of next 2 sts; rep from * to last 5 sts, 3sc in next sc, 1sc in each of next 2 sts, sc2tog.

Row 54: Change to D, 1ch (does not count as a st), skip first st, sc2tog, 1sc in next st, *3sc in next st, (center of 3-sc), 1sc in each of foll 2 sts, sc3tog, 1sc in each of next 2 sts; rep from * to last 5 sts, 3sc in next sc, 1sc in each of next 2 sts, sc2tog.

Row 55: Change to B, 3ch (does not count as a st), skip first st, 1tr in next st, *1dc in foll st, 1hdc in next st, 1sc in foll st, 1hdc in next st, 1dc in foll st, tr3tog; rep from * to last 6 sts, 1dc in next st, hdc2tog, turn leaving last 3 sts unworked.

Row 56: Change to C, 1ch (counts as first st), skip first st, 1sc in each st to end.

Row 57: Change to D, 1ch (counts as first st), skip first st, 1sc in each st to end, 1sc in 1-ch.

All sizes:

Do not turn after Row 57.

Row 58: With RS facing, attach A, 3ch (counts as first dc), skip first st, 1dc in each st to end. (19:**21**:25 sts)

Row 59: Skip first st, *1dc in next st, ss in foll st; rep from * to end, working last ss in top of 3-ch. (18:**20**:24 sts)

Row 60: 3ch (counts as first dc), skip first st, 1dc in each st to end, ending 1dc in last 1-dc.

Row 61: Skip first st, ss in next st, *1dc in foll st, ss in next st; rep from * to end, working last ss in top of 3-ch. (17:**19**:23 sts)

Row 62: 3ch (counts as first dc), skip first st, 1dc in each st to end, ending 1dc in last ss.

Row 63: Skip first st, *1dc in next st, ss in foll st; rep from * to end, working last ss in top of 3-ch. (16:**18**:22 sts)

Row 64: 3ch (counts as first dc), skip first st, 1dc in each st to end, ending 1dc in last 1-dc.

Row 65: 3ch (counts as first dc), skip first st, ss in next st, *1dc in foll st, ss in next st; rep from * working last ss in top of 3-ch.

Row 66: 3ch (counts as first dc), skip first st, 1dc in each st to end, 1dc in top of 3-ch from previous row.

Rows 67–68: Rep Rows 65–66.

Fasten off.

Right Front

Work as for left front, reversing all shaping.

sleeves

(Make 2)

Using A, make 35ch. Begin working Floret Patt.

Row 1 (RS): 1dc in 4th ch from hook and each ch to end. (33 sts)

Row 2: 1ch (counts as first st), skip first st, *1dc in foll st, ss in next st; rep from * working last ss in top of 3-ch.

Row 3: 3ch (counts as first dc), skip first st, 1dc in each st to end, working last dc in 1-ch.

Row 4 (inc row): 3ch (counts as first dc), ss in first st, *1dc in next st, ss in next st; rep from * to end, ending ss and 1dc in top of 3-ch (1 st inc at each end). (35 sts)

Row 5: 3ch (counts as first dc), skip first st, 1dc in each st to end, working last dc in top of 3-ch.

Row 6: 3ch (counts as first st), skip first st, *ss in next st, 1dc in next st; rep from * working last dc in top of 3-ch.

Row 7 (inc row): 3ch (counts as dc), 1dc in first st, 1dc in each st to end, 2dc in 1-ch (1 st inc at each end). (37:37:37 sts)

Row 8: As Row 2.

Row 9: As Row 3.

Rep Rows 4–9 until work has 55:55:55 sts. (34:34:34 rows in total)

Row 35 (RS): 1sc in each st to end. (55:55:55 sts)

Rows 36–47: Work Wave-&-Chevron Patt. (9:9:9 Wave reps)

Do not turn after Row 47. Cont in Floret Patt.

Row 48: With RS facing attach A, 3ch (counts as first dc), skip first st, 1dc in each st to end. (55:55:55 sts)

Row 49: 1ch (counts as first st), skip first st, *1dc in next st, ss in foll st; rep from * to end, working last ss in top of 3-ch.

Row 50: 3ch (counts as first dc), skip first st, 1dc in each st to end, working last dc in 1-ch.

Rep Rows 49–50 twice more, then work Row 49 again.

Fasten off.

Finishing

With RS together, sew shoulder and side seams. Sew sleeve seams from cuff edge to last 3 rows, leaving these open to inset sleeve in body. Sew sleeves in armholes.

Sleeve edging:

Using A and with RS facing, work 1sc in other side of each foundation chain of sleeve cuffs, join with ss in first sc, turn. (33 sc)

Work 4 rounds of sc, turning at end of each round.

Edging and buttonhole band:

Using A, with RS facing and starting at bottom edge of left front, work 1sc in the other side of each foundation chain of bottom edges of left front, back, and right front, 3sc in right front corner, work sc evenly up front edge

in ends of rows, keeping work flat, sc around back neck and down left front to starting point, working 3sc in left front corner, join with ss in first sc, turn.

Work 2 rounds of sc, working 3sc in center sc at lower corners and turning at the end of each round.

Buttonhole round: Make 5 buttonholes in right front evenly spaced between bottom edge and beginning of neckline shaping as foll: work sc to buttonhole position, 2ch, skip 1sc in previous round, cont in sc to end, ss in first sc, turn.

Round 5: 1sc in each st, working 2sc in each 2-ch space for buttonhole, ss in first sc.

Fasten off.

Sew buttons onto left front to match buttonholes.

Collar

With RS facing, attach A to sc edging just above top buttonhole on right front where neckline shaping begins, work a row of sc up right front neck, across back neck, and down left front neck, stopping at corresponding point just above top button on opposite side; turn.

Next row (WS): Skip first st, 1sc in each st to end, turn.

Cont working backward and forward, dec 1 st at the start of every row, until collar measures 6½in. (16cm) from Row 1 of Edging and buttonhole band.

PETER PAN COLLAR CARDIGAN

** skill level

THIS DELICATE CARDIGAN HAS SUCH A PRETTY COLLAR. THE COLORS GIVE IT THAT "VINTAGE" FEEL, AS DOES THE CHARMING SHELL STITCH USED.

MATERIALS

50% baby alpaca/50% merino mix sport (babyweight) yarn, such as Rooster Almerino Baby

>> 8:8 x 1¾oz (50g) balls—approx 1096:**1096**yd (1000:**1000**m)—of blue-green (A)

>> 1:1 x 1¾oz (50g) ball—approx 125:**125**m (137:**137**yd)— of off-white (B)

US size E/4 (3.5mm) crochet hook

5 buttons, ¾in. (17mm) in diameter

Abbreviations

ch chain
cont continue
dc double crochet
hdc half double crochet
patt pattern
rep repeat
RS right side
sc single crochet
sp(s) space(s)
ss slip stitch
st(s) stitch(es)
WS wrong side

Gauge

2 patt repeats (14 sts) and 8 rows measure 3¼in. (8cm) over patt using US size E/4 (3.5mm) hook.

Size

To fit sizes:

	10–12	**14–16**

Finished measurements

Bust		
in.	85	101
cm	33½	39¾
Length to back neck		
in.	20½	21¼
cm	52	54
Sleeve length		
in.	12	12
cm	30	30

Right Front

Using A, make 39:**46**ch.

Row 1 (RS): 1dc in 4th ch from hook, *skip 2 ch, 5dc (1 shell) in next ch, skip 2 ch, 1dc in each of next 2 ch (pair of dc); rep from * to end.

Row 2: 3ch, 2dc in first dc, *1dc in sp between 2nd and 3rd dc of shell, 1dc in sp between 3rd and 4th dc of shell, 1 shell between pairs of dc; rep from * ending pair of dc in last shell, 3dc in sp between last dc and 3-ch.

Row 3: 3ch, 1dc between first 2 dc, *1 shell between pair of dc, 1 pair dc in next shell; rep from * ending 1dc in sp between last dc and 3-ch, 1dc in 3rd of 3-ch, turn.

Rows 2 and 3 set patt.

Row 4. As Row 2.

Row 5: Work in patt to last 3 sts, 1dc in sp between last 2 sts.

Row 6: 3ch, skip 3 sts, patt to end.

Row 7: Patt to last st, 1dc in top of 3-ch.

Row 8: 3ch, skip 3 sts, 1dc in next sp, patt to end.

Row 9: Patt ending 1 pair dc in last shell, 3dc in last sp.

Row 10: 3ch, 1dc between first 2 dc, skip 3 dc, 1 shell between pairs of dc, patt to end.

Rows 11–16: Rep Rows 9 and 10 3 times more.

Shape waist:

Row 17: Patt to last sp, 4dc in last sp.

Row 18: 3ch, 1dc in first sp, 2dc in next sp, patt to end.

Cont in patt until work measures approx 11¾:**12½**in. (30:**32**cm), ending at front edge.

Shape armhole:

Row 1: Patt to last full shell, 1 pair dc in center of shell, turn.

Row 2: Patt to end.

Row 3: Patt ending 1 shell between last pair of dc, 1dc in sp after last dc.

Row 4: 3ch, skip 3 sts, patt to end.

Row 5: Patt ending 4dc between last pair of dc, 1dc in top of 3-ch.

Row 6: 3ch, 1dc in between 3rd and 4th dc, patt to end.

Row 7: Patt to last sp, 2dc in sp before turning ch.

Shape neck:

Row 1: 3ch, skip first 2 dc, 4dc between pair of dc, patt to last 8:**15** sts, 1dc between 2nd and 3rd dc of shell, turn.

Row 2: 3ch, 1dc between 2nd and 3rd dc of shell, patt to last 6 sts, 1dc in center of shell, 1dc in top of 3-ch.

Row 3: 3ch, 1dc in sp, patt to last 4 sts, 1dc in top of 3-ch.

Row 4: 3ch, patt to last pair of dc, 4dc in sp between pair of dc, 1dc in top of 3-ch.

Row 5: 3ch, 1dc between 2nd and 3rd dc of shell, patt to last st, 1dc in top of 3-ch.

Row 6: 3ch, 3dc between pair of dc, pair of dc in next shell, 3dc in last sp.

Row 7: 3ch, 1dc in first sp, 1 shell in pair of dc, 1dc in next sp, 1dc in top of 3-ch.

Row 8: 3ch, 1dc in next sp, 1 pair dc in shell, 2dc in last sp.

Row 9: 3ch, 1 shell, 1dc in last sp.

Row 10: 3ch, 1 pair dc in shell, 1dc in top of 3ch.

Row 11: 3ch, 3dc between pair of dc, 1dc in last sp.

Row 12: 3ch, skip 2 dc, 1dc in sp before each of next 2 dc, 1dc in top of 3-ch.

Row 13: 3ch, 1dc between pair of dc, 1dc in last sp.

Row 14: 3ch, 2dc in last sp.

Row 15: 3ch, 1dc in last sp.

Fasten off.

Left Front

Work as for right front, reversing shaping.

Back

Using A, make 81:**95**ch and work first 4 rows as for right front.

Row 5: 3ch, 1 shell in first pair of dc, patt to last 3 sts, 1dc in sp between last 2 sts.

Row 6: 3ch, 1 pair dc in next shell, patt to last st, 1dc in top of 3-ch.

Row 7: 3ch, 1 shell between pair of dc, patt to last pair dc, 1 shell, 1dc in top of 3-ch.

Row 8: 3ch, skip 3 sts, 1dc in next sp, patt to last shell, 1dc between 3rd and 4th dc, 1dc in top of 3-ch.

Row 9: As Row 2.

Row 10: 3ch, 1dc in first sp, 1 shell in first pair of dc, patt to end, ending 1 shell in last pair of dc, 1dc in last sp, 1dc in 3rd of 3-ch.

Rows 11–16: Rep Rows 9 and 10 three times more.

Row 17: 3ch, 3dc in first sp, patt to end, 4dc in last sp.

Row 18: 3ch, 1dc in first sp, 2dc in next sp, patt to last 4 dc, skip 2 dc, 2dc in next sp, 2dc in last sp.

Cont in patt until work measures same length as front to armhole, ending with a WS row.

Shape armholes:

Row 1: Ss over 6 sts, ss in next sp, 3ch, 1dc in next sp, patt to last full shell, 1 pair dc in center of shell, turn.

Row 2: Patt to end.

Row 3: 3ch, skip first 3 dc, 1 shell between pair of dc, patt to end, ending 1 shell in last pair of dc, 1dc in 3rd of 3-ch.

Row 4: 3ch, 1 pair of dc in next shell, patt to end, ending 1 pair of dc in last shell, 1dc in top of 3-ch.

Row 5: 3ch, 4dc in pair of dc, patt to last 3 sts, 4dc between last pair of dc, 1dc in top of 3-ch.

Row 6: 3ch, skip 3 dc, 1dc in next sp, patt to last 5 sts, skip 2 dc, 1dc in next sp, 1dc in top of 3-ch.

Row 7: 3ch, 1dc in first sp, 1 pair of dc in first shell, patt to last 2 sts, 1dc in last sp, 1dc in top of 3-ch.

Row 8: As Row 5.

Rep Rows 6–8 three:**four** times more, then work Rows 6–7 again.

1st size only:

Patt 3 rows even.

Both sizes:

Fasten off.

Sleeves

(Makes 2)

Using A, make 39:**46**ch and work 5 rows in patt as right front.

Row 6: 3ch, 3dc in first sp, patt to end, 4dc in last sp.

Row 7: 3ch, 1dc in next sp, 1dc in each of next 2 sps, patt to last 4 sts, 1dc in each of next 2 sps, 2dc in last sp.

Row 8: 3ch, 1dc, skip next sp, 3dc in next sp, patt to last 4 sts, 3dc in next sp, 2dc in last sp.

Row 9: 3ch, 1dc in sp, skip next sp, 1dc in each of next 2 sps, patt to last 5 sts, 1dc in each of next 2 sps, skip 1 sp, 2dc in last sp.

Rows 10–13: Rep Rows 8–9 twice more.

Row 14: 3ch, 1dc in first sp, skip next sp, 1 shell in next sp, patt to last 2 sts, 2dc in 3rd of 3-ch.

Work 4 rows in patt as set.

Row 19: 3ch, 3dc in first sp, patt to end, ending 3dc in last sp, 1dc in 3rd of 3-ch.

Row 20: 3ch, 2dc in first sp, 1dc in next sp, patt to last 4 sts, skip next sp, 1dc in next sp, 2dc in last sp, 1dc in 3rd of 3-ch.

Rows 21–26: Work Rows 8–9 three times.

Row 27: As Row 3.

Row 28: As Row 2.

Rows 29–30: As Rows 27–28.

Shape armholes:

Row 1: Ss over 7 sts, ss in next sp, 3ch, 1dc in next sp, patt to last full shell, 1 pair of dc in shell, turn.

Rep Rows 2–7 of shape armholes section on back.

Row 8: As Row 5.

Row 9: As Row 6.

Row 10: 3ch, 2dc in sp, patt to last sp, 2dc in sp, 1dc in top of 3-ch.

Row 11: 3ch, 1dc in 2nd sp, patt to last 3 dc, 1dc between 2 dc, 1dc in top of 3-ch.

Row 12: 3ch, skip 1 sp, 1dc in next sp, patt to last 2 sts, 1dc in sp, 1dc in top of 3-ch.

Row 13: 3ch, 1dc in first sp, patt to last sp, 2dc in last sp.

Row 14: 3ch, skip 1 sp, 1dc in next sp, patt to last 2 dc, 1dc in sp before 2 dc, 1dc in top of 3-ch.

Row 15: 3ch, patt to last 2 dc, 1dc in top of 3-ch.

Row 16: 3ch, patt to last dc, 1dc in top of 3-ch.

Row 17: 3ch, 3dc in first pair dc, patt to last pair dc, 3dc, 1dc in top of 3-ch.

Row 18: 3ch, 1dc in 2nd sp, patt to last 3 dc, 1dc in 2nd sp, 1dc in top of 3-ch.

Row 19: 3ch, patt to last 2 dc, 1dc in top of 3-ch.

Row 20: 3ch, 3dc in first pair dc, patt to last 3 sts, 3dc in next pair dc, 1dc in top of 3-ch.

Row 21: 3ch, 1dc in 2nd sp, patt to last 4 sts, 1dc in sp between 2nd and 3rd sts, 1dc in top of 3-ch.

Row 22: 3ch, 1dc in first sp, patt to last st, 1dc in last sp, 1dc in top of 3-ch.

Fasten off.

Set in sleeves, join side and sleeve seams.

Collar

Using B, work 114:**142**sc all around neck edge.

Row 1: 2ch, skip first sc, 1hdc in next sc, *3ch, skip 2 sc, 1sc in next sc, 3ch, skip 2 sc, 1hdc in each of next 2 sts; rep from * to end, turn.

Row 2: 2ch, skip first hdc, 1hdc in next hdc, *3ch, skip 3 ch, [1sc, 3ch, 1sc] in next sc (1 crown made), 3ch, skip 3 ch, 1hdc in each of 2 hdc; rep from * working last hdc in 2nd of 2-ch.

Row 3: 1ch, skip first hdc, 1sc in next hdc, *1sc in 3-ch sp, 5ch, skip crown, 1sc in next 3ch sp, 1sc in each of 2 hdc; rep from *, working last sc in 2nd of 2-ch.

Row 4: 1ch, skip 1 sc, 1sc in next sc, *skip 1 sc, 7sc in 5-ch sp, skip 1 sc, 1sc in each of next 2 sc; rep from * working last sc in 1-ch.

Row 5: 2ch, skip 1 sc, 1hdc in next sc, *3ch, skip 3 sc, 1sc in next sc, 3ch, skip 3 sc, 1hdc in each of next 2 sc; rep from *, working last hdc in 1-ch.

Rep Rows 2–5 once more, then Rows 2–4 again.

Fasten off.

Edging

Using A, and starting at top of left front, work 2sc in each row end to bottom corner, work 5sc in corner, work 2sc in each sp along bottom edge and 1sc in base of each shell, work 5sc in last sp, then work 2sc in each row end along right front.

Fasten off.

Finishing

Use holes in pattern as buttonholes and sew on buttons to correspond.

Sew in ends.

skill level

THIS BEADED CARDIGAN IS IN MOHAIR MIXED WITH SILK, WHICH MAKES IT A REALLY SOFT YARN TO WEAR. IT ALSO COMES IN SOME REALLY SCRUMPTIOUS COLORS.

BEADED CARDIGAN

MATERIALS

76% super kid mohair/24% silk lace laceweight yarn, such as Debbie Bliss Angel

>> 5:**5**:6:**6** x ⅞oz (25g) balls—approx
1094:**1094**:1313:**1313**yd
(1000:**1000**:1200:**1200**m)—of pale pink

1100:**1200**:1200:**1300** Debbie Abrahams size 6 beads shade white

1½yd (130cm) of ⅜-in.- (9-mm-) wide double-faced satin ribbon

Sewing needle and thread to match ribbon

US size G/6 (4mm) crochet hook

Abbreviations

ch chain

cont continue

dc double crochet

dec decrease(d)

patt pattern

rem remaining

rep repeat

RS right side

sc single crochet

ss slip stitch

st(s) stitch(es)

Special abbreviations

PB place bead

V-st (V stitch) [1dc, 1ch, 1dc] in required space.

DV-st (double V stitch) [2dc, 1ch, 2dc] in required space.

Gauge

19 sts x 9 rows over 4in. (10cm) square over V-st Patt using US size G/6 (4mm) hook.

Size

To fit sizes:

	8	10	12	14

Finished measurements

To fit bust

	8	10	12	14
in.	33½	**34¾**	38½	**39¾**
cm	85	**88**	98	**101**
Length				
in.	20	**20**	20	**20**
cm	51	**51**	51	**51**
Sleeve				
in.	12¼	**12¼**	12¼	**12¼**
cm	31	**31**	31	**31**

Back

Make 82:**88**:94:**100**ch.

Row 1 (RS): V-st in 5th ch from hook, *skip 2 ch, V-st in next ch; rep from * to last 2 ch, skip 1 ch, 1dc in last ch, turn. (26:**28**:30:**32** V-sts)

Row 2: 3ch, skip 2 sts, DV-st in ch sp at center of next V-st, *PB, 1ch, skip next V-st, DV-st in ch sp at center of next V-st; rep from * to last V-st, PB, 1ch, skip V-st, 2dc in top of 3-ch.

Row 3: 3ch, V-st in each ch sp to end, 1dc in top of 3-ch.

Row 4: 3ch, 1dc in first st, *PB, 1ch, skip next V-st, DV-st in ch sp at center of next V-st; rep from * to end leaving last loop of last dc of last DV-st on hook and working it together with 1dc in top of 3-ch.

Row 5: Rep Row 3.

Rep Rows 2–5 until back measures 19¾:**19¾**:19¾:**19¾**in. (50:**50**:50:**50**cm). Fasten off.

Right Front

Make 43:**43**:49:**49**ch.

Work first row of patt as for back. (13:**13**:15:**15** V-sts)

Row 2: 3ch, skip 2 sts, DV-st in ch sp at center of next V-st, *PB, 1ch, skip next V-st, DV-st in ch sp at center of next V-st; rep from * leaving last loop of last dc of last DV-st on hook and working it together with 1dc in top of 3-ch.

Row 3: 3ch, V-st in each ch sp to end, 1dc in top of 3-ch.

Row 4: 3ch, 1dc in first st, *PB, 1ch, skip next V-st, DV-st in ch sp at center of next V-st; rep from * to last st, PB, 1ch, skip V-st, 2dc in top of 3-ch.

Row 5: Rep Row 3.

Rep Rows 2–5 until front measures 12¼:**12¼**:12¼:**12¼**in. (31:**31**:31:**31**cm), ending with a Row 5.

Shape neck:

Row 1: 3ch, skip 2 sts, DV-st in ch sp at center of next V-st, *PB, 1ch, skip next V-st, DV-st in ch sp at center of next V-st; rep from * 3:**3**:4:**4** times more, PB, 1ch, skip next V-st, 2dc in ch sp at center of next V-st, turn.

Row 2: 3ch, V-st in each ch sp to end, 1dc in top of 3-ch.

Row 3: Patt as set, ending 2dc in last 1-ch sp, turn.

Rep Rows 2 and 3 until 14:**14**:17:**17** sts rem.

Cont even until right front measures same as back. Fasten off.

Left Front

Work as for right front to neck shaping.

Shape neck:

Row 1: Break yarn, skip first 2 V-sts, rejoin yarn in 1-ch sp at center of next V-st, 3ch, 1dc in same place, work patt as set to end. Complete to match right front, reversing shaping. Fasten off.

Sleeves

(Make 2)

Make 82:**88**:88:**94**ch.

Work in patt as for back (26:**28**:28:**30** V-sts) until sleeve measures 11¾:**11¾**:11¾:**11¾**in. (30:**30**:30:**30**cm). Fasten off.

Finishing

Join shoulder seams.

Measure 8¼:**8⅞**:8¾:**9½**in. (21:**22.5**:22.5:**24**cm) either side of shoulder seam and mark. Sew in sleeves between markers.

Join side and sleeve seams

Picot Edging

Join yarn to bottom corner of left front, 1ch, 1sc in ch at base of first dc, 1sc in ch sp, *[1sc, 1ch, PB, 1ch, 1sc] in ch at base of V-st, 2sc in 2-ch sp; rep from * all along bottom edge, then spacing edging evenly, work up right front, around neck edge, and down left front; join with ss in first sc. Work edging around lower edge of sleeves.

Cut ribbon into 2 equal lengths and sew to WS of last row of front before neck shaping.

MOTIF SWEATER 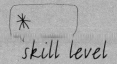 *skill level*

EMBELLISHMENTS LOOK GREAT ON VINTAGE-STYLE
SWEATERS AND CAN REALLY LIVEN UP A SIMPLE GARMENT.
THE BEADED SWIRLS ON THE SHOULDERS
WERE PURCHASED READY MADE AND
HAND SEWN TO THE FINISHED SWEATER.

Abbreviations

ch chain

cont continue

hdc half double crochet

hdc2tog half double crochet
2 stitches together

rem remain

rep repeat

RS right side

sc single crochet

st(s) stitch(es)

WS wrong side

Gauge

15 sts x 13 rows over 4in. (10cm) square
working hdc using US size G/6 (4mm) hook.

Size

To fit sizes:

	8–10	10–12	12–14

Finished measurements

To fit bust

	8–10	10–12	12–14
in.	32–33	**34–35**	36–37
cm	80–83	**85–88**	90–93

Actual measurement

in.	35¾	**39¼**	44
cm	91	**100**	112

Length

in.	21½	**21½**	21½
cm	55	**55**	55

Sleeve seam length

in.	18	**18**	18
cm	46	**46**	46

MATERIALS

76% super kid mohair/24% silk lace
laceweight yarn, such as Debbie Bliss Angel

>> 8 x ⅞oz (25g) balls—approx 1750yd
(1600m)—of orange

2 sew-on beaded motifs for shoulders

US size G/6 (4mm) crochet hook

Back

Make 69:**76**:85ch.

Row 1: 1hdc in 3rd ch from hook, 1hdc in each ch to end. (68:**75**:84 sts)

Row 2: 2ch, 1hdc in each st to end.

Rep Row 2 until back measures 19½:**19½**:19½in. (50:**50**:50cm).

Fasten off.

Front

Work as for back until front measures 13:**13**:13in. (33:**33**:33cm).

Shape neck:

Work first 30:**34**:38 sts, turn.

Cont on these sts only, working hdc2tog at neck edge on every row until 17:**18**:19 sts rem.

Cont even until front measures same as back.

Fasten off.

Skip center 8:**7**:8 sts, rejoin yarn to next st, and work to end.

Work as for first side.

Fasten off.

Sleeves

(Make 2)

Make 37:**39**:41ch.

Work in hdc as for back, working 2hdc at each end of every 3rd row until there are 66:**68**:70 sts.

Work even until sleeve measures 16¼:**16¼**:16¼in. (41:**41**:41cm).

Fasten off.

Finishing

Sew up shoulder seams.

Fold sleeve in half WS together, place fold to shoulder seam, and sew in sleeves.

Sew sleeve and side seams.

Bottom edging:

Join yarn at side seam at bottom edge, *1sc in each of next 2 sts, skip 1 st; rep from * all around bottom edge.

Cont working in rounds of sc until bottom edging measures 2in. (5cm).

Fasten off.

Cuffs:

Join yarn to seam at lower edge of sleeve, *1sc in each of next 3 sts, skip next st; rep from * all around cuff edge.

Cont working in rounds of sc until cuff measures 2in. (5cm).

Fasten off.

Neck edging:

Work sc evenly all around neck edge.

Cont working in rounds of sc until neck edging measures 2:**2**:2in. (5:**5**:5cm).

Fasten off.

Sew in ends.

Stitch on beaded motif at front of each shoulder.

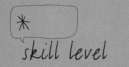
THIS PATCHWORK CARDIGAN IS MADE WITH CIRCLES INSTEAD OF TRADITIONAL SQUARES. THERE ARE LOTS LIKE IT IN VINTAGE MARKETS, BUT MAKING YOUR OWN IS MUCH MORE SATISFYING!

CIRCLES CARDIGAN

MATERIALS

50% baby alpaca/50% merino mix sport (babyweight) yarn, such as Rooster Almerino Baby
>> 6 x 1¾oz (50g) balls—approx 822yd (750m)—of shade off-white (A)
>> 1 x 1¾oz (50g) ball—approx 137yd (125m)—each of shade beige (B), aquamarine (C), green (D), red (E)

55% merino/33% microfiber/12% cashmere light worsted (DK) yarn, such as Debbie Bliss Baby Cashmerino
>> 1 x 1¾oz (50g) ball—approx 137yd (125m)—each of navy (F), deep pink (G)

US size E/4 (3.5mm) crochet hook

Abbreviations
ch chain
dc double crochet
hdc half double crochet
rep repeat
sp(s) space(s)
ss slip stitch
st(s) stitch(es)
yo yarn over hook

Special abbreviation
puff st [yo, insert hook in ring, yo and pull through] twice, yo and pull through all 5 loops on hook.

Gauge
Each circle measures approx 3⅛in. (8cm) diameter.

Size
One size.

Finished measurements
Bust: 37¾in. (96cm)
Length: 23½in. (60cm)
Sleeve seam: 15in. (38cm)

Circles

(make 128)

Use either B, C, D, E, F, or G for Rounds 1, 2, and 3, changing color at the end of each round, and A for Round 4. Using first color, make 4ch, join with ss to form a ring.

Round 1: 3ch, 1hdc in ring (counts as first puff st), 1ch, [puff st, 1ch] 7 times in ring, join with ss in hdc. (8 petals) Fasten off.

Round 2: Attach next color in any 1-ch sp, 3ch, 1dc in next ch sp, 2ch, [2dc, 2ch] in each of next 7 ch sps, join with ss in top of 3-ch.

Fasten off.

Round 3: Attach next color in any 2-ch sp, 3ch, [1dc, 1ch, 2dc, 1ch] in same ch sp, [2dc, 1ch] twice in each of next 7 ch sps, join with ss in top of 3-ch.

Fasten off.

Round 4: Attach A in any 1-ch sp, 3ch, 2dc in same ch sp, 1ch, [3dc, 1ch] in each of next 15 ch sps, join with ss in top of 3-ch.

Fasten off.

Finishing

Sew in ends.

Join circles through corresponding pairs of 3-dc.

For each front, join 7 rows each of 3 circles. For back, join 8 rows each of 6 circles. Join fronts to back at shoulders (top row of back circles sits halfway across shoulders).

Join 1 row of 5 circles for top of first sleeve, then add 2 rows of 4 circles and 2 rows of 3 circles. Join center circle of 5-circle row of sleeve to circle on shoulder and 2 circles on either side to corresponding circles on back or front. Join side/sleeve seam. Rep for sleeve on other side.

Shape neck:

Turn 1st and 2nd circles at front neck edge under by approx one half, sew, and press to create a neck edge.

CROCODILE SHAWL

THIS IS A GREAT FALL/WINTER SHAWL MADE USING AN UNUSUAL CROCODILE STITCH, WHICH GIVES THE LOOK OF SCALES. TIED WITH A PRETTY VINTAGE RIBBON AT THE FRONT, IT MAKES A GREAT ACCESSORY FOR A LIGHT TEA DRESS.

Abbreviations
ch chain
cont continue
dc double crochet
rep repeat
sc single crochet
sp space
ss slip stitch
st(s) stitch(es)
yo yarn over hook

Gauge
3 scales x 9 rows over 4in. (10cm) square using size US size G/6 (4.5mm) crochet hook.

Size
One size.

Finished measurement
Widest point: 47in. (119.5cm)
Deepest point: 11in. (28cm)

Tips
When working the scale stitch, it's easier to turn your work to the side when working round the stalks. When each scale is completed, the WS of doubles are on the RS of the shawl.

The scales are made in every alternate 2-dc group.

MATERIALS
50% baby alpaca/50% merino mix sport (babyweight) yarn, such as Rooster Almerino Baby
>> 6 x 1¾oz (50g) balls—approx 822yd (750m)—of off-white

US size G/6 (4.5mm) crochet hook

60in. (1.5m) of 1¼-in.- (3-cm-) wide ribbon

Scale Stitch Pattern

Yo, insert hook in next 2-ch sp and bring hook from back to front through center of 2-dc group (around back of first stalk), yo and complete dc, make 4 more dc around same stalk, 1ch (working around 2nd stalk of 2-dc group), yo, insert hook in next 2-ch sp, bring hook from back to front of 2nd stalk through center of same 2-dc group, yo, pull yarn through and complete dc; keeping Row 1 (sc row) to your right, make 4 more dc around same stalk. (1 scale made)

Shawl

Beginning at lower edge, make 96ch.

Row 1 (RS): 1sc in 2nd ch from hook, 1sc in each ch to end. (95 sts)

Row 2: 3ch, 1dc in base of 3-ch (counts as 1 pair dc) *2ch, skip next 2 sts, 1dc in each of next 2 sts (2-dc group worked); rep from * to last 3 sts, 2ch, skip 2 sts, 2dc in last st.

Row 3: *Yo, insert hook from back to front in center of 2-dc group, yo, pull yarn through, complete dc; rep from * 4 times more. 1ch (working around 2nd stalk of 2-dc group), yo, insert hook in next 2-ch sp, bring hook from back to front of 2nd stalk through center of same 2-dc group, yo, pull yarn through and complete dc; keeping Row 1 (sc row) to your right, make 4 more dc around same stalk (1 scale made), skip next 2-dc group, **yo, insert hook in next 2-ch sp and bring hook from back to front through center of 2-dc group (around back of first stalk), yo and complete dc; make 4 more dc round same stalk, 1ch (working around 2nd stalk of 2-dc group), yo, insert hook in next 2-ch sp, bring hook from back to front of 2nd stalk through center of same 2-dc group, yo, pull yarn through and complete dc; keeping Row 1 (sc row) to your right, make 4 more dc around same stalk (1 scale made), skip next 2-dc group; rep from ** ending 1 scale in last 2-dc group. (12 scales)

Row 4: 3ch, 1dc in top of last dc of scale from previous row, *2ch, 2dc in center of next scale, 2ch, 2dc in center of next 2-dc group from Row 2; rep from * to last scale, 2dc in center of last scale, 2ch, 2dc in top of last dc of scale from previous row.

Rep Rows 3 and 4 until 33 scales have been made across one row, finishing on a Row 3.

Next row: 3ch, *2dc in center of next scale, 2ch, 2dc in center of next 2-dc group; rep from * ending 2dc in center of last scale.

Next row: Rep Row 3, omitting last scale, ending 1sc in second of 3-ch from previous row.

Next row: 2dc in center of first 2-dc group, 2ch, *2dc in center of next scale, 2ch, 2dc in center of next 2-dc group; rep from * ending 2dc in last scale.

Next row: Rep Row 3.

Fasten off.

Finishing

Sew in ends.

Cut ribbon in half and stitch one piece to each short end of shawl.

Tweed skirt
shorts
Cotton Dress
Wool Dress

Tweed skirt

shorts

SKIRTS, SHORTS & DRESSES

Cotton Dress

Wool Dress

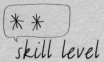

** *skill level*

A GREAT LITTLE SKIRT MADE USING A SMART AND EFFECTIVE TWEED STITCH IN THREE VIVID COLORS.

TWEED SKIRT

Special abbreviations
fpdc (front post double) dc worked around stalk of st from previous round from front of work
bpdc (back post double) dc worked around stalk of st from previous round from back of work

Gauge
22 sts x 21 rows over 4in. (10cm) square working Tweed st using US size G/6 (4mm) hook.

MATERIALS
50% baby alpaca/50% merino mix light worsted (DK) yarn, such as Rooster Almerino DK
>> 2:**2**:3:**3** x 1¾oz (50g) balls—approx 248:**248**:372:**372**yd (225:**225**:337.5:**337.5**m)—of dark blue (A)
>> 2:**2**:2:**2** x 1¾oz (50g) balls—approx 248:248:248:248yd (225:**225**:225:**225**m)—each of yellow (B), red (C)

US size G/6 (4mm) crochet hook

Size
To fit sizes:

	8	10	12	14

Finished measurements
Hips/Waist

	8	10	12	14
in.	28	30	31½	33½
cm	71	76	80	85
Length				
in.	16	16	16	16
cm	41	41	41	41

Abbreviations
beg begin	**RS** right side
ch chain	**sc** single crochet
cont continue	**sp** space
dc double crochet	**st(s)** stitch(es)
foll follows	**WS** wrong side
hdc half double crochet	**yo** yarn over hook
inc increase/increasing	
rep repeat/repeating	

Skirt Front & Back

(make 2 the same)

Using A make 55:**61**:65:**71**ch.

Row 1 (RS): Skip 2 ch, 1hdc in each ch to end.
(54:**60**:64:**70** sts)

Row 2: 2ch, skip first st, *fpdc around stalk of next st,
1bpdc around stalk of next st; rep from * to last st, 1hdc in
top of 2-ch.

Row 3: 2ch, skip first st, *1bpdc around stalk of next st,
1fpdc around stalk of next st; rep from * to last st, 1hdc in
top of 2-ch.

Inc row: 1ch, skip first st, working in sc inc 24 sts evenly
across. (78:**84**:88:**94** sts)

Beg working Tweed st as foll:

Row 5: 1ch, 1sc in first st, *1ch, skip 1 st, 1sc in next st;
rep from * to last sc, 1sc in last sc.

Do not fasten off; attach B.

Row 6: Using B, 1ch, 1sc in first st, *1ch, skip 1 st, 1sc in
next ch sp; rep from * to last sc, 1sc in last sc.

Do not fasten off; attach C.

Row 7: Using C, rep Row 6.

Cont to change color in this sequence, rep Row 6 to form
Tweed st, until work measures 16in. (41cm).

Fasten off.

Finishing

With WS together, sew up side seams, and turn RS out.
Block and press.

Tip

The skirt is designed to sit on the hips, rather
than at the waist.

CROCHET SHORTS ARE VERY TRENDY.
IF YOU PREFER A LONGER LEG,
THEN SIMPLY ADD MORE ROWS.

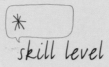
skill level

SHORTS

MATERIALS

100% cotton light worsted (DK) yarn, such as Rowan Cotton Glace

>> 4 x 1¾oz (50g) balls—approx 503yd (460m)—of green (A)
>> 1 x 1¾oz (50g) ball—approx 126yd (115m)—of ecru (B)

1⅜yd (120cm) of ⅜-in.- (8-mm-) wide satin ribbon

US size D/3 (3mm) crochet hook

Abbreviations

ch chain
cont continue
dc double crochet
rep repeat
RS right side
sc single crochet
sp space
ss slip stitch
st(s) stitch(es)

Size

To fit sizes:

	8–10	12–14

Finished measurements

Hips		
in.	33	37¾
cm	84	95
Length		
in.	11¾	11¾
cm	30	30

Gauge

19 sts x 11½ rows over 4in. (10cm) square working dc using US size D/3 (3mm) hook.

Shorts Legs

(make 2 the same)
Using A, make 98:**108**ch.
Row 1: 1dc in 3rd ch from hook, 1dc in each ch to end. (96:**106** sts)
Rows 2–6: 3ch, 1dc in each st to end. (96:**106** sts)
Fasten off.
Row 7: Skip 5 sts, rejoin A in 6th st from end, 3ch, 1dc in each st to last 5 sts, turn, leaving last 5 sts unworked. (86:**96** sts)
Row 8: Working on these sts only, 3ch, 1dc in each st to end.
Cont working in dc until work measures 9¾in. (24.5cm) or length desired.
Eyelet row: 3ch, *skip 1 st, 1dc in each of next 6 sts, 1ch; rep from * to end.
Next row: 3ch, *1dc in next ch sp, 1dc in each st to next ch sp; rep from * to end.
Next row: 1ch, 1sc in each st to end.
Fasten off.

Finishing

With RS together, join pieces (seams will be at the front and back).
Top edging:
With RS facing, attach A in front seam at top, 1ch, 1sc in each st around top, join with ss in first ch.
Fasten off.
With RS facing, attach B in first sc of last round, 1sc in same st, *2ch, skip 2 sts, 1dc in next st, 2ch, 4dc in 2-ch sp just made, skip 2 sts, 1sc in next st; rep from * to end, skipping 1sc at end of last rep, join with a ss in first sc.
Fasten off.
Leg edging:
With RS facing, join B in any st around first leg bottom, *2ch, skip 2 sts, 1dc in next st, 2ch, 4dc in 2-ch sp just made, skip 2 sts, 1sc in next st; rep from * to end, skipping 1sc at end of last rep, join with ss in first of sc.
Fasten off.
Rep on 2nd leg.
Thread ribbon through eyelets to tie at center front.

* * *
skill level

A GREAT SUMMER GARMENT TO WEAR OVER JEANS OR LEGGINGS. IT'S DEFINITELY ONE FOR THE COMMITTED CROCHETER, BUT WORTH THE WORK.

COTTON DRESS

Abbreviations
ch chain
dc double crochet
hdc half double crochet
rep repeat
RS right side
sc single crochet
sp(s) space(s)
ss slip stitch
st(s) stitch(es)
WS wrong side
yo yarn over hook

Special abbreviation
4dcCL (4 double cluster) yo, insert hook in ch sp, [yo, draw loop through, yo, draw through 2 sts] 4 times (5 loops on hook), yo, draw through all 5 loops (1 cluster)

Gauge
23 sts x 10 rows over 4in. (10cm) square working pattern using US size D/3 (3mm) hook.

Size
To fit sizes:

	8–10	10–12	12–14
To fit bust			
in.	32–33	34–35	36–37
cm	81–84	85–89	90–94

Finished measurements
Length excluding straps

in.	32¼	32¼	32¼
cm	82	82	82
Length with straps			
in.	35½	35½	35½
cm	90	90	90

MATERIALS
100% cotton crochet yarn, such as DMC Natura Just Cotton
>> 11:**12**:13 x 1¾oz (50g) balls—approx 1864.5:**2034**:2203.5yd (1705:**1860**:2015m)—of off-white

US size D/3 (3mm) crochet hook

Front & Back

(make 2 the same)

Make 273:**285**:297ch.

Row 1 (WS): 1dc in 5th ch from hook (counts as first dc and 1 ch sp), *1ch, skip 1 ch, 1dc in next ch; rep from * to end. (271:**283**:295 sts)

Row 2: 1ch (counts as first sc), *sc in ch sp, 1ch; rep from * to 4-ch, 1sc in ch sp, 1sc in 3rd ch.

Row 3: 4ch (counts as first dc and 1 ch sp), skip 2 sc, [1dc in next ch sp, 1ch] until 129:**135**:141 sts have been worked, 1ch, skip 1 sc, 1dc in each of next 11 sts, 1ch, skip 1 sc, [1dc in next ch sp, 1ch] to last sc, skip last sc, 1dc in 1-ch.

Row 4: 4ch, skip 1 ch sp and 1 dc, [1dc in next ch sp, 1ch] until 129:**135**:141 sts have been worked, 2ch, skip next 2 dc, 1dc in each of next 7 dc, 2ch, skip next 2 dc, [1dc in next ch sp, 1ch] to last 3 sts, 1ch, 1dc in 3rd of 4 ch. (269:**281**:293 sts)

Row 5: 4ch, skip 1 ch sp and 1 dc, [1dc in next ch sp, 1ch] until 125:**131**:137 sts have been worked, 2 ch, skip 1 dc and 1 ch sp, 1dc in next dc, 2dc in 2-ch sp, 2ch, skip next 2 dc, 1dc in each of next 3 dc, 2ch, skip next 2 dc, 2dc in 2-ch sp, 1dc in next dc, 2ch, skip 1 ch sp and 1 dc, [1dc in next ch sp, 1ch] to last 3 sts, 1dc in 3rd of 4-ch. (267:**279**:291 sts)

Row 6: 4ch, skip 1 ch and 1 dc, [1dc in next ch sp, 1ch] until 121:**127**:133 sts have been worked, 2ch, skip next dc and ch sp, 1dc in next dc, 2dc in 2-ch sp, 1dc in each of next 3dc, 2dc in 2-ch sp, 3ch, 2dc in next 2-ch sp, 1dc in each of next 3 dc, 2dc in next 2-ch sp, 1dc in next dc, 2ch, skip next ch sp and dc, [1dc in next ch sp, 1ch] to last 3 sts, skip last dc and ch sp, 1dc in 3rd of 4-ch. (265:**277**:289 sts)

Row 7: 4ch, skip 1 ch and 1 dc, [1dc in next ch sp, 1ch] until 120:**126**:132 sts have been worked, 2dc in 2-ch sp, 1dc in each of next 8 dc, 3dc in 3-ch sp, 1dc in each of next 8 dc, 2dc in 2-ch sp, 1ch, skip 1 dc, [1dc in next ch sp, 1ch] to last 3 sts, skip last dc and ch sp, 1dc in 3rd of 4-ch. (263:**275**:287 sts)

Row 8: 4ch, skip 1 dc and 1 ch sp, [1dc in next ch sp, 1ch] until 120:**126**:132 sts have been worked, skip 1 dc, 1dc in each of next 9 dc, 3ch, skip next 3 dc, 1dc in each of next 9 dc, 1ch, skip next dc, [1dc in next ch sp, 1ch] to last 3 sts, skip last dc and ch sp, 1dc in 3rd of 4-ch. (261:**273**:285 sts)

Row 9: 4ch, skip 1 ch sp and 1 dc, [1dc in next ch sp, 1ch] until 120:**126**:132 sts have been worked, skip 1 dc, 1dc in each of next 6 dc, 2ch, skip next 2 dc, 3dc in 3-ch sp, 2ch, skip next 2 dc, 1dc in each of next 6 dc, 1ch, skip 1 dc, [1dc in next ch sp, 1ch] to last 3 sts, skip 1 dc and 1 ch sp, 1dc in 3rd of 4-ch. (259:**271**:283 sts)

Row 10: 4ch, skip 1 ch sp and 1dc, [1dc in next ch sp, 1ch] until 120:**126**:132 sts have been worked, skip 1 dc, 1dc in each of next 3 dc, 2ch, skip next 2 dc, 2dc in next 2-ch sp, 1dc in each of next 3 dc, 2dc in 2-ch sp, 2ch, skip 2 dc, 1dc in each of next 3 dc, 1ch, skip 1 dc, [1dc in next ch sp, 1ch] to last 3 sts, skip 1 dc and ch sp, 1dc in 3rd of 4-ch. (257:**269**:281 sts)

Row 11: 4ch, skip 1 ch sp and 1 dc, [1dc in next ch sp, 1ch] until 120:**126**:132 sts have been worked, skip 1 dc, 1dc in next dc, 1ch, skip 1 dc, 2dc in 2-ch sp, 1dc in each of next 7 dc, 2dc in 2-ch sp, 1ch, skip 1 dc, 1dc in next dc, 1ch, skip next dc, [1dc in next ch sp, 1ch] to last 3 sts, skip 1 dc and 1 ch sp, 1dc in 3rd of 4-ch. (255:**267**:279 sts)

Row 12: 4ch, skip 1 ch and 1 dc, [1dc in next ch sp, 1ch] until 122:**128**:134 sts have been worked, skip 1 dc, 1dc in each of next 9 dc, 1ch, skip 1 dc, [1dc in next ch sp, 1ch] to last 3 sts, skip 1 dc and 1 ch sp, 1dc in 3rd of 4-ch. (253:**265**:277 sts)

Row 13: 4ch, skip 1 ch sp and 1 dc, [1dc in next ch sp, 1ch] until 122:**128**:134 sts have been worked, skip 1 dc, 1dc in each of next 7 dc, 1ch, skip 1 dc, [1dc in next ch sp, 1ch] to last 3 sts, skip 1 dc and 1 ch sp, 1dc in 3rd of 4-ch. (251:**263**:275 sts)

Row 14: 4ch, skip 1-ch sp and 1 dc [1dc in next ch sp, 1ch] until 122:**128**:134 sts have been worked, skip 1 dc, 1dc in each of next 5 dc, 1ch, skip next dc, [1dc in next ch sp, 1ch] to last 3 sts, skip 1 dc and 1 ch sp, 1dc in 3rd of 4-ch. (249:**261**:273 sts)

Row 15: 4ch, skip 1 ch sp and 1 dc, [1dc in next ch sp, 1ch] until 122:**128**:134 sts have been worked, skip 1 dc, 1dc in each of next 3 dc, 1ch, skip 1 dc, [1dc in next 1-ch sp, 1ch] to last 3 sts, 1dc in 3rd of 4-ch. (247:**259**:271 sts)

Row 16: 4ch, skip 1 ch sp and 1 dc, [1dc in next ch sp, 1ch] until 122:**128**:134 sts have been worked, skip 1 dc, 1dc in next dc, 1 ch, skip next dc, [1dc in next ch sp, 1ch] to last 3 sts, 1dc in 3rd of 4-ch. (245:**257**:269 sts)

Row 17: 4ch, skip 1 ch sp and 1 dc, [1dc in next ch sp, 1ch] to last 3 sts, skip 1 dc and 1 ch sp, 1dc in 3rd of 4-ch. (243:**255**:267 sts)

Row 18: Rep Row 17. (241:**253**:265 sts)

Row 19: 4ch, skip 1 ch sp and 1 dc, [1dc in next ch sp, 1ch] until 67:**73**:79 sts have been worked, *2ch, skip 1 dc and 1 ch sp, 1dc in next dc, 1dc in each of next ch sp and dc, 2ch, skip 1 ch sp and 1dc**, [1dc in next ch sp, 1ch] until 91 sts have been worked; rep from * to ** once, [1dc in next ch sp, 1ch] to last 3 sts, 1dc in 3rd of 4-ch. (239:**251**:263 sts)

Row 20: 4ch, skip 1 ch sp and 1 dc, [1dc in next ch sp, 1ch] until 63:**69**:75

Note

1dc and 1ch = 2 sts.

In Rows 4–55, every row will be decreased by 1 st at each end.

Every row that starts with 4ch—1dc and 1ch = first 2 sts.

Row 23: 4ch, skip 1 ch sp and 1 dc, [1dc in next ch sp, 1ch] until 51:**57**:63 sts have been worked, *2ch, skip 1 dc and ch sp, 1dc in next dc, 2dc in 2-ch sp, 1dc in each of next 3 dc, 2dc in 2-ch sp, 2ch, skip next 2 dc, 1dc in each of next 7 dc, 2ch, skip next 2 dc, 2dc in 2-ch sp, 1dc in each of next 3dc, 2dc in 2-ch sp, 1dc in next dc, 2ch, skip 1 ch sp and 1 dc**, [1dc in next ch sp, 1ch] until 67 sts have been worked; rep from * to ** once, [1dc in next ch sp, 1ch] to last 3 sts, skip 1 dc and 1 ch sp, 1dc in 3rd of 4-ch. (231:**243**:255 sts)

Row 24: 4ch, skip 1 ch sp and 1dc, [1dc in next ch sp, 1ch] until 50:**56**:62 sts have been worked, *2dc in 2-ch sp, 1dc in each of next 8 dc, 2dc in 2-ch sp, 2ch, skip next 2 dc, 1dc in each of next 3 dc, 2ch, skip 2 dc, 2dc in 2-ch sp, 1dc in each of next 8 dc, 2dc in 2-ch sp, 1ch**, [1dc in next ch sp, 1ch] until 66 sts have been worked; rep from * to ** once, [1dc in next ch sp, 1ch] to last 3 sts, skip 1 dc and 1 ch sp, 1dc in 3rd of 4-ch. (229:**241**:253 sts)

Row 25: 4ch, skip 1 ch sp and 1 dc, [1dc in next ch sp, 1ch] until 48:**54**:60 sts have been worked, *1dc in next 1 ch sp, 1dc in each of next 12 dc, 2dc in 2-ch sp, 3ch, skip next 3 dc, 2dc in 2-ch sp, 1dc in each of next 12 dc, 1dc in 1 ch sp, 1ch**, [1dc in next ch sp, 1ch] until 64 sts have been worked; rep from * to ** once, [1dc in next ch sp, 1ch] to last 3 sts, skip 1 dc and 1 ch sp, 1dc in 3rd of 4-ch. (227:**239**:251 sts)

Row 26: 4ch, skip 1 ch sp and 1 dc, [1dc in next ch sp, 1ch] until 48:**54**:60 sts have been worked, *skip 1dc, 1dc in each of next 13 dc, 1ch, skip 1 dc, 3dc in 3-ch sp, 1ch, skip 1 dc, 1dc in each of next 13 dc, 1ch, skip 1 dc**, [1dc in next ch sp, 1ch] until 66 sts have been worked; rep from * to ** once, [1dc in next ch sp, 1ch] to last 3 sts, skip 1 dc and 1 ch sp, 1dc in 3rd of 4-ch. (225:**237**:249 sts)

Row 27: 4ch, skip 1 ch sp and 1 dc, [1dc in next ch sp, 1ch] until 48:**54**:60 sts have been worked, **skip 1 dc, 1dc in each of next 11 dc, 1ch, skip 1 dc, 1dc in 1-ch sp, 1dc in each of next 3 dc, 1dc in next 1-ch sp, 1ch, skip 1 dc, 1dc in each of next 11 dc, 1ch, skip 1 dc**, [1dc in next ch sp, 1ch] until 68 sts have been worked; rep from * to ** once, [1dc in next ch sp, 1ch] to last 3 sts, skip 1 dc and 1 ch sp, 1dc in 3rd of 4-ch. (223:**235**:247 sts)

Row 28: 4ch, skip 1 ch sp and 1 dc, [1dc in next ch sp, 1ch] until 48:**54**:60 sts have been worked, *skip 1 dc, 1dc in each of next 9 dc, 1ch, skip 1 dc, 1dc in 1-ch sp, 1dc in each of next 5 dc, 1dc in 1-ch sp, 1ch, skip 1 dc, 1dc in each of next 9 dc, 1ch, skip 1 dc**, [1dc in next ch sp, 1ch] until 70 sts have been worked; rep from * to ** once, [1dc in next ch sp, 1ch] to last 3 sts, skip 1 dc and 1 ch sp, 1dc in 3rd of 4-ch. (221:**233**:245 sts)

Row 29: 4ch, skip 1 ch sp and 1 dc, [1dc in next ch sp, 1ch] until 48:**54**:60 sts have been worked, *skip 1 dc, 1dc in each of next 7 dc, 1ch, skip 1 dc, 1dc in 1-ch sp, 1dc in each of next 7 dc, 1dc in 1-ch sp, 1ch, skip 1 dc, 1dc in each of next 7 dc, 1ch, skip next dc**, [1dc in next ch sp, 1ch] until 72 sts have been worked; rep from * to ** once, [1dc in next ch sp, 1ch] to last 3 sts, 1dc in 3rd of 4-ch. (219:**231**:243 sts)

sts have been worked, *2ch, skip 1 dc and 1 ch sp, 1dc in next dc, 2dc in 2-ch sp, 1dc in each of next 3 dc, 2dc in 2-ch sp, 1dc in next dc, 2ch, skip 1 ch sp and 1 dc**, [1dc in next ch sp, 1ch] until 85 sts have been worked; rep from * to ** once, [1dc in next ch sp, 1ch] to last 3 sts, skip 1 dc and 1 ch sp, 1dc in 3rd of 4-ch. (237:**249**:261 sts)

Row 21: 4ch, skip 1 ch sp and 1 dc, [1dc in next ch sp, 1ch] until 59:**65**:71 sts have been worked, *2ch, skip 1 dc and 1 ch sp, 1dc in next dc, 2dc in 2-ch sp, 1dc in each of next 9 dc, 2dc in 2-ch sp, 1dc in next dc, 2ch, skip 1 ch sp and 1 dc**, [1dc in next ch sp, 1ch] until 79 sts have been worked; rep from * to ** once, [1dc in next ch sp, 1ch] to last 3 sts, skip 1 dc and 1 ch sp, 1dc in 3rd of 4-ch. (235:**247**:259 sts)

Row 22: 4ch, skip 1 ch sp and 1 dc, [1dc in next ch sp, 1ch] until 55:**61**:67 sts have been worked, *2ch, skip 1 dc and 1 ch sp, 1dc in next dc, 2dc in 2-ch sp, 2ch, skip next 2 dc, 1dc in each of next 11 dc, 2ch, skip next 2 dc, 2dc in 2-ch sp, 1dc in next dc, 2ch, skip 1 ch sp and 1 dc**, [1dc in next ch sp, 1ch] until 73 sts have been worked; rep from * to ** once, [1dc in next ch sp, 1ch] to last 3 sts, skip 1 dc and 1 ch sp, 1dc in 3rd of 4-ch. (233:**245**:257 sts)

Row 30: 4ch, skip 1 ch sp and 1 dc, [1dc in next ch sp, 1ch] until 48:**54**:60 sts have been worked, *skip 1 dc, 1dc in each of next 5 dc, 1ch, skip 1 dc, 1dc in 1-ch sp, 1dc in each of next 9 dc, 1dc in 1-ch sp, 1ch, skip 1 dc, 1dc in each of next 5 dc, 1ch, skip next dc**, [1dc in next ch sp, 1ch] until 74 sts have been worked; rep from * to ** once, [1dc in next ch sp, 1ch] to last 3 sts, skip 1 dc and 1 ch sp, 1dc in 3rd of 4-ch. (217:**229**:241 sts)

Row 31: 4ch, skip 1 dc and 1 ch sp, [1dc in next ch sp, 1ch] until 48:**54**:60 sts have been worked, *skip 1 dc, 1dc in each of next 3 dc, 1ch, skip 1 dc, 1dc in 1-ch sp, 1dc in each of next 11 dc, 1dc in 1-ch sp, 1ch, skip 1 dc, 1dc in each of next 3 dc, 1ch, skip next dc**, [1dc in next ch sp, 1ch] until 76 sts have been worked; rep from * to ** once, [1dc in next ch sp, 1ch] to last 3 sts, 1dc in 3rd of 4-ch. (215:**227**:239 sts)

Row 32: 4ch, skip 1 ch sp and 1 dc, [1dc in next ch sp, 1ch] until 48:**54**:60 sts have been worked, *skip 1 dc, 1dc in next dc, 1ch, skip next dc, 1dc in 1-ch sp, 1dc in each of next 13 dc, 1dc in 1-ch sp, 1ch, skip 1 dc, 1dc in next dc, 1ch, skip next dc**, [1dc in next ch sp, 1ch] until 78 sts have been worked; rep from * to ** once, [1dc in next ch sp, 1ch] to last 3 sts, 1dc in 3rd of 4-ch. (213:**225**:237 sts)

Row 33: 4ch, skip 1 ch sp and 1 dc, [1dc in next ch sp, 1ch] until 50:**56**:62 sts have been worked, *skip 1 dc, 1dc in each of next 13 dc, 1ch, skip next dc**, [1dc in next ch sp, 1ch] until 84 sts have been worked; rep from * to ** once, [1dc in next ch sp, 1ch] to last 3 sts, skip 1 dc and 1 ch sp, 1dc in 3rd of 4-ch. (211:**223**:235 sts)

Row 34: 4ch, skip 1 ch sp and 1 dc, [1dc in next ch sp, 1ch] until 50:**56**:62 sts have been worked, *skip 1 dc, 1dc in each of next 11 dc, 1ch, skip next dc**, [1dc in next ch sp, 1ch] until 86 sts have been worked; rep from * to ** once, [1dc in next ch sp, 1ch] to last 3 sts, skip 1 dc and 1 ch sp, 1dc in 3rd of 4-ch. (209:**221**:233 sts)

Row 35: 4ch, skip 1 ch sp and 1 dc, [1dc in next ch sp, 1ch] until 50:**56**:62 sts have been worked, *skip 1 dc, 1dc in each of next 9 dc, 1ch, skip next dc**, [1dc in next ch sp, 1ch] until 88 sts have been worked; rep from * to ** once, [1dc in next ch sp, 1ch] to last 3 sts, skip 1 dc and 1 ch sp, 1dc in 3rd of 4-ch. (207:**219**:231 sts)

Row 36: 4ch, skip 1 ch sp and 1 dc, [1dc in next ch sp, 1ch] until 50:**56**:62 sts have been worked, *skip 1 dc, 1dc in each of next 7 dc, 1ch, skip next dc**, [1dc in next ch sp, 1ch] until 90 sts have been worked; rep from * to ** once, [1dc in next ch sp, 1ch] to last 3 sts, skip 1 dc and 1 ch sp, 1dc in 3rd of 4-ch. (205:**217**:229 sts)

Row 37: 4ch, skip 1 ch sp and 1 dc, [1dc in next ch sp, 1ch] until 50:**56**:62 sts have been worked, *skip 1 dc, 1dc in each of next 5 dc, 1ch, skip next dc**, [1dc in next ch sp, 1ch] until 92 sts have been worked; rep from * to ** once, [1dc in next ch sp, 1ch] to last 3 sts, skip 1 dc and 1 ch sp, 1dc in 3rd of 4-ch. (203:**215**:227 sts)

Row 38: 4ch, skip 1 ch sp and 1 dc, [1dc in next ch sp, 1ch] until 50:**56**:62 sts have been worked, *skip 1 dc, 1dc in each of next 3 dc, 1ch, skip next

dc**, [1dc in next ch sp, 1ch] until 94 sts have been worked; rep from * to ** once, [1dc in next ch sp, 1ch] to last 3 sts, skip 1 dc and 1 ch sp, 1dc in 3rd of 4-ch. (201:**213**:225 sts)

Row 39: 4ch, skip 1 ch sp and 1 dc, [1dc in next ch sp, 1ch] until 50:**56**:62 sts have been worked, *skip 1 dc, 1dc in next dc, 1ch, skip next dc**, [1dc in next ch sp, 1ch] until 96 sts have been worked; rep from * to ** once, [1dc in next ch sp, 1ch] to last 3 sts, skip 1 dc and 1 ch sp, 1dc in 3rd of 4-ch. (299:**211**:223 sts)

Row 40: 4ch, skip 1 ch sp and 1 dc, [1dc in next ch sp, 1ch] to last 3 sts, skip 1 dc and 1 ch sp, 1dc in 3rd of 4-ch. (197:**209**:221 sts)

Rows 41–55: Rep Row 40. (167:**179**:191 sts)

Begin working cluster pattern:

Note: On Row 56, work 4dcCL over 3 ch sps, working 1 st in first ch sp, 2 sts in 2nd ch sp and 1 st in 3rd ch sp.

Row 56 (RS): 2ch, [4dcCL over next 3 ch sps, 5ch, skip 1 ch sp] 2:**4**:6 times, [4dcCL over next 3 ch sps, 5ch, skip 2 ch sps] 12:**10**:8 times, [4dcCL over next 3 ch sps, 5ch, skip 1 ch sp] 3:**5**:7 times, 4dcCL over last 3 ch sps, 1hdc in 3rd of 4-ch. (105:**117**:129 sts)

Row 57: 7ch (counts as first hdc and 5ch), *4dcCL in next 5-ch sp, 5ch; rep from * to end, 1hdc in top of 2-ch.

Row 58: 2ch (counts as first hdc), *4dcCL in 5-ch sp, 5ch; rep from * to last 5-ch sp, 4dcCL in ch sp, 1hdc in top of 2-ch.

Rows 59–60: Rep Rows 57–58.

Row 61: 4ch, [1dc and 1ch in first 4dcCL] 0:1:1 time, *[1dc, 1ch 1dc] in next 5-ch sp, 1ch, 1dc in top of cluster, 1ch, [1dc, 1ch, 1dc] in 5-ch sp, 1ch, skip next 4dcCL; rep from * to end, ending [1dc, 1ch] in last ch sp, [1dc and 1ch in last 4dcCL] 0:0:1 time, 1dc in 2nd of 2-ch. (87:**99**:111 sts)

Bodice:

Row 62: 3ch, 1dc in first ch sp, 1ch, *1dc in next ch sp, 1ch; rep from * to last 4-ch, 1dc in ch sp, 1dc in 3rd of 4-ch.

Row 63: 4ch, skip 1 dc, *1dc in next ch sp, 1ch; rep from * to last dc, skip 1 dc, 1dc in top of 3-ch.

Row 64: Rep row 62.

Row 65: 4ch, skip 1 dc, [1dc in next ch sp, 1ch] until 43:**49**:55 sts have been worked, 1dc in next dc, [1dc in next ch sp, 1ch] to last dc, skip 1 dc, 1dc in top of 3-ch.

Row 66: 3ch, 1dc in first ch sp, 1ch, [1dc in next ch sp, 1ch] until 36:**42**:48 sts have been worked, 1dc in next dc, 1dc in next ch sp, 3ch, skip 1 dc and ch sp and next dc, 1dc in next ch sp, 1dc in each of next 3 dc, 1dc in ch sp, 3ch, skip 1 dc and ch sp and next dc, 1dc in next ch sp, 1dc in next dc, [1dc in next ch sp, 1ch] to last 4 ch, 1dc in ch sp, 1dc in 3rd of 4-ch. Fasten off.

Shape armholes:

Row 67: Skip first 6 sts, attach yarn to next ch sp, 4ch, [1dc in next ch sp, 1ch] until 29:**35**:41 sts have been worked, 1dc in each of next 2 dc, 3ch, skip 1 dc, 1dc in 3-ch sp, 1dc in each of next 5 dc, 1dc in 3-ch sp, 3ch, skip 1 dc, 1dc in each of next 2 dc, [1dc in next ch sp, 1ch] to last 6 sts, turn. (75:**87**:99 sts)

Row 68: 3ch, 1dc in first ch sp, 1ch, [1dc in next ch sp, 1ch] until 28:**34**:40 sts have been worked, 1dc in each of next 2 dc, 3ch, skip next dc, 1dc in 3-ch sp, 1dc in each of next 7 dc, 1dc in 3-ch sp, 3ch, skip 1 dc, 1dc in each of next 2 dc, [1dc in next ch sp, 1ch] to last 4 ch, 1dc in ch sp, 1dc in 3rd of 4-ch.

Row 69: 4ch, skip 1 dc, [1dc in next ch sp, 1ch] until 27:**33**:39 sts have been worked, 1dc in each of next 2 dc, 3ch, skip 1 dc, 1dc in 3-ch sp, 1dc in each of next 9 dc, 1dc in 3-ch sp, 3ch, skip 1 dc, 1dc in each of next 2 dc, [1dc in next ch sp, 1ch] to last dc, skip 1 dc, 1dc in top of 3-ch.

Rows 68–69 set pattern for central V. Keeping pattern correct as set, widening central V shape by 1 st at each side on every row, work a further 8 rows.

Row 78: 3ch, 1dc in each st to end. (75:**87**:99 sts)

Row 79: 1dc in each dc to end.

Row 80: Work 1 row of sc, skipping every 3rd st. Fasten off.

Straps

(make 2)

Make 48ch.

Row 1 (WS): 1dc in 4th ch from hook, 1dc in each ch to end. (46 sts)

Row 2: 3ch, 1dc in each dc to end, turn.

Rep last row once more.

Row 4: *3ch, skip 1 dc, ss in next dc; rep from * to end. Fasten off.

Finishing

With RS together, sew up side seams, turn RS out. Fold over last 2 rows of bodice to RS and sew down very carefully.

Sew straps to top of bodice, placing straight edge to armhole edge.

Armhole edging

Attach yarn at underarm seam, 3ch, work 1 round of dc evenly all around armhole and straps, ss to 3rd of 3-ch.

Next round: 3ch, 1dc in each dc to end, ss in 3rd of 3-ch.

Next round: Work as for Row 4 of straps. Fasten off.

Fold over last 2 rows to RS and sew down neatly.

Hem edging

Attach yarn in first ch sp after side seam, work 3ch, 3dc in same sp, skip 2 sps, *4dc in next sp, 3ch, skip 2 ch sps; rep from * all around the hem, ss to top of 3-ch. Fasten off.

Next round: Rejoin yarn to last dc of first set of 4 sts, *15ch, skip 2 sets of 4-dc, ss in first dc of next set of 4-dc, 3ch, ss in same dc, skip 1 dc, ss in sp between 2nd and 3rd dc, 3ch, ss in same sp, skip next dc, ss in 4th dc, 3ch, ss in same dc; rep from * all around hem, ss in first of 15-ch. Fasten off.

THIS STYLISH LITTLE DRESS IS MADE USING SIMPLE HERRINGBONE DOUBLE STITCH. THE SLEEVES ARE THREE-QUARTER LENGTH, BUT MAKE THEM—AND THE DRESS—LONGER IF YOU PREFER.

WOOL DRESS

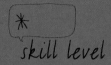
skill level

MATERIALS

50% baby alpaca/50% merino mix light worsted (DK) yarn, such as Rooster Almerino DK

>> 12 x 1¾oz (50g) balls—approx 1488yd (1350m)—of gray (A)
>> 1 x 1¾oz (50g) ball—approx 124yd (112.5m)—of orange (B)

US size D/3 (3mm) and US size E/4 (3.5mm) crochet hooks

Small piece of fabric for pocket lining

Abbreviations
ch chain
cont continue
dc double crochet
patt pattern
rep repeat
RS right side
sc single crochet
ss slip stitch
st(s) stitch(es)
WS wrong side
yo yarn over hook

Special abbreviation
HBdc (Herringbone double) yo, insert hook, yo, draw through st and first loop on hook, yo, draw through 1 loop, yo, draw through both loops on hook
Patt row: 3ch (counts as 1dc), skip 1 st, 1HBdc in next and each st to end, working last st in top of 3-ch. Rep Patt row.

Gauge
16 sts x 8 rows over 4in. (10cm) square working HBdc patt using US size E/4 (3.5mm) hook.

Size
To fit sizes:

	8	10	12	14	16

Finished measurements
Bust

	8	10	12	14	16
in.	33½	36¼	38¼	40¼	42¼
cm	85	92.5	97.5	102.5	107.5
Length					
in.	31¾	31¾	31¾	32	32
cm	80.5	80.5	80.5	81.5	81.5
Sleeve					
in.	12	12	12	12	12
cm	30	30	30	30	30

Back

Using E/4 (3.5mm) hook and A, make 97:**97**:105:**105**:113ch.
Row 1: 1sc in 2nd ch from hook, 1sc in each ch to end.
(96:**96**:104:**104**:112 sts)
Row 2: 1ch (counts as first sc), skip first st, 1sc in next and each st
to end.
Cont in HBdc patt, work 4:**3**:6:**3**:6 rows.
Start dec 1 st at each end of next and every foll 3rd:**4th**:3rd:**4th**:4th row
until you have 68:**74**:78:**82**:86 sts.
Work even until work measures 23½in. (60cm).
Fasten off.
Shape armholes:
Skip first 6 sts, rejoin yarn in next st and work across row to last 6 sts,
turn. (56:**62**:66:**70**:74 sts)
Work even until armhole measures 7¼:**7¼**:7¼:**7½**:7½in. (18:**18**:18:**19**:19cm).
Shape neck:
Work across first 12:**15**:17:**17**:19 sts, turn.
Work one more row on these sts.
Fasten off.
Skip center 32:**32**:32:**36**:36 sts.
Rejoin yarn to next st and work as for first side.

Front

Work as for back until armholes measure 2in. (5cm).
Shape neck:
Work first 23:**26**:28:**29**:31 sts, turn.
Working on this first set of sts, dec 1 st at neck edge on every row to
12:**15**:17:**17**:19 sts.
Work even until armhole measures same as back.
Fasten off.
Skip center 10:**10**:10:**12**:12 sts, rejoin yarn in next st and work 2nd side of
neck to match first side.

Sleeves

(Make 2)
Using E/4 (3.5mm) hook and B, make 49:**49**:53:**53**:57ch.
Row 1: 1sc in 2nd ch from hook, 1sc in each ch to end.
(48:**48**:52:**52**:56 sts)
Row 2: 1ch, 1sc in each st to end.
Rep Row 2 for ¾ in. (2cm).
Change to A, work in HBdc as for back, inc 1 st (2HBdc in same st) at each
end of 2nd and every alt row to 64:**64**:68:**68**:72 sts.

Work even until sleeve measures 12in. (30cm).
Fasten off.
Shape top:
Skip next 6 sts, rejoin yarn in next st, and work across the row to last
6 sts. (55:**52**:56:**56**:60 sts)
Fasten off.
With RS together, join shoulder seams.
Neck edge:
Using E/4 (3.5mm) hook and B, work 26 sc down left front, 10:**10**:10:**12**:12
sc across front, 26 sts up right front, 4 sts down right back, 32:**32**:32:**36**:36
sts across back, 4 sts up left back, ss in first st. (102:**102**:102:**108**:108 sc)
Working in rounds, work 1sc in each st until neck edge measures ⅞in. 2cm).
Fasten off.

Pocket

Using D/3 (3mm) hook and B, make 22ch.
Row 1: 1sc in 2nd ch from hook, 1sc in each ch to end. (21 sts)
Row 2: 1ch, 1sc in each st to end. (21 sts)
Rep Row 2 until pocket measures 4in. (10cm).
Fasten off.

Finishing

Sew in sleeves and
join sleeve and side
seams. Sew in ends.
Line WS of pocket
with fabric and sew
onto dress.

Block Color Pillow

Tassel Pillow

BAGS & PILLOWS

slouch Bag

Tassel Pillow
slouch Bag
Patchwork Bag
Block Color Pillow

Patchwork Bag

A FUN AND FLUFFY THROW PILLOW, CROCHETED IN HALF DOUBLES. IT TAKES A WHILE TO ATTACH THE TASSELS, BUT THE RESULT IS WORTH THE EFFORT.

TASSEL PILLOW

MATERIALS

50% baby alpaca/50% merino wool mix worsted (Aran) yarn, such as Rooster Almerino Aran

>> 12 x 1¾oz (50g) balls—approx 1236yd (1128m)—of coral

US size E/4 (3.5mm) crochet hook

16-in. (41-cm) square pillow form

Abbreviations
ch chain
hdc half double crochet
rep repeat
sc single crochet
st(s) stitches
WS wrong side

Gauge
18 sts x 13 rows over 4in. (10cm) square working hdc using US size E/4 (3.5mm) hook.

Finished measurement
Fits 16-in. (41-cm) square pillow form.

Front & Back

(make 2 the same)
Make 69ch.
Row 1: 1hdc in 2nd ch from hook, 1hdc in each ch to end. (68 sts)
Row 2: 2ch, 1hdc in each st to end. (68 sts)
Rep Row 2 until work measures 16in. (41cm).
Fasten off.

Finishing

With two pieces WS together, use sc seam to join along sides and bottom, making 3sc in each corner stitch. Insert pillow form, close top of pillow using a sc seam.
Fasten off.

Tassels

Wrap yarn around 4 fingers 4 times, break yarn. Cut loops at one end to form tassel. Insert crochet hook in one hdc on pillow front, catch folded end of tassel with hook, pull all eight strands through st by approx 1in. (2.5cm); keeping hook in same loop catch cut ends of tassel and pull through loop. Take out hook and pull yarn ends with fingers to tighten tassel. Continue looping tassels in this way in every other st, until pillow is completely covered with tassels. Trim all tassels to one length.

SLOUCH BAG

THIS IS A BIG BAG, JUST PERFECT FOR WEEKEND ESSENTIALS, AND THE TEXTURED STITCH REALLY HIGHLIGHTS THE COLORS.

MATERIALS

50% baby alpaca/50% merino mix light worsted (DK) yarn, such as Rooster Almerino DK

>> 5 x 1¾oz (50g) balls—approx 620yd (562.5m)—of off-white (A)

>> 3 x 1¾oz (50g) balls—approx 372yd (337.5m)—of orange (B)

US size G/6 (4mm) crochet hook

Fabric for lining, optional

Gauge
2 patts measure 4in (10cm) and 8 rows measure 3⅛in. (8cm) working Catherine Wheel st using US size G/6 (4mm) hook.

Finished measurement
Approx 15 x 16½in. (38 x 42cm)

Abbreviations
ch chain
dc double crochet
dtr double treble
patt(s) pattern(s)
rep repeat
RS right side
sc single crochet
ss slip stitch
st(s) stitch(es)
tr treble
WS wrong side
yo yarn over hook

Special abbreviation
CL (cluster) *yo, insert hook in next st, yo, pull yarn through, yo, pull through 2 loops, work from * to * over the number of sts given on patt rows, yo and pull through all loops on hook.

Front & Back

(make 2 the same)

Using A, make 77ch.

Row 1: 1sc in 2nd ch from hook, 1sc in next ch, *skip 3 ch, 7dc in next ch, skip 3 ch, 1sc in each of next 3 ch; rep from * to last 4 ch, skip 3 ch, 4dc in last ch.

Fasten off A, attach B.

Row 2 (RS): 1ch, 1sc in each of first 2 sts, *3ch, 1CL over next 7 sts, 3ch, 1sc in each of next 3 sts; rep from * to last 4 sts, 3ch, 1CL over last 4 sts.

Row 3: 3ch (counts as 1dc), 3dc in top of 4dcCL, *skip 3 ch, 1sc in each of next 3 sc, skip 3 ch, 7dc in closing loop of next CL; rep from * to end, finishing skip 3 ch, 1sc in each of last 2 sc.

Fasten off B, attach A.

Row 4: 2ch (counts as 1dc) skip first st, 1CL over next 3 sts, *3ch, 1sc in each of next 3 sts, 3ch, 1CL over next 7 sts; rep from * to end, finishing 3ch, 1sc in next st, 1sc in top of 3-ch from previous row.

Row 5: 1ch, 1sc in each of first 2 sc, *skip 3 ch, 7dc in closing loop of next CL, skip 3 ch, 1sc in each of next 3 sc; rep from * to end, finishing skip 3 ch, 4dc in top of 2-ch from previous row.

Fasten off A, attach B.

Rep Rows 2–5 until work measures approx 16in. (40cm), ending on a Row 2.

Fasten off.

Edging:

With RS facing, join A in corner st at top right edge, 1ch, 2sc in same st, 1sc in each st across top to next corner, 3sc in corner st, sc evenly down first side (approx 70 sc), 3sc in corner st, 1sc in each ch along bottom edge, sc evenly up 2nd side to match sts on first side.

Sides/Strap

Using A, make a chain 75in. (190cm) long.

Row 1: 1sc in 2nd ch from hook, 1sc in each ch to end.

Row 2: 1ch, 1sc in each st to end.

Rep Row 2 until the piece measures 3in. (7.5cm).

Fasten off.

Rose

Using B, make 99ch.

Petals 1–4: Skip 3 ch, 1dc in each of next 2 ch, 2ch, ss in next ch, [3ch, 1dc in each of next 2 ch, 2ch, ss in next ch] 3 times.

Petals 5–8: [4ch, 1tr in each of next 4 ch, 3ch, ss in next ch] 4 times.

Petals 9–12: [4ch, 1tr in each of next 6 ch, 3ch ss in next ch] 4 times.

Petals 13–16: [5ch, 1dtr in each of next 8ch, 4ch, ss in next ch] 4 times.

Fasten off.

Starting with smaller petals, coil petals keeping base flat at ch edge and stitching in place as you go along.

Finishing

If the bag is to be lined, use front, back, and sides/strap as templates to cut fabric, allowing extra ½in. (1cm) all round for seams.

Mark center of long edges of sides/strap with pins. Match pin marker to center bottom of front. Pin and join one edge of side section to edge of front around bottom and two sides, using either sc seam or hand stitching. Rep on other side, attaching back to other edge of side section.

With WS together, join ends of strap section using hand stitching.

Attach rose to top of bag near one strap.

Make up fabric lining as for bag and hand stitch inside bag and along strap.

PATCHWORK BAG

skill level ✗ ✗

THIS PATCHWORK BAG IS MADE IN BRIGHT SQUARES AND STRIPES SET AGAINST WHITE. A FABRIC LINING WILL MAKE THE BAG STRONGER, BUT IS NOT ESSENTIAL.

MATERIALS

50% baby alpaca/50% merino wool mix worsted (Aran) yarn, such as Rooster Almerino Aran

>> 3 x 1¾oz (50g) balls—approx 309yd (282m)—of off-white (A)

>> 1 x 1¾oz (50g) ball—approx 103yd (94m)—each of green (B), bright pink (C), purple (D), red (E), yellow (F), deep blue (G)

100% Peruvian highland wool light worsted (DK) yarn, such as Cascade 220

>> 1 x 3½oz (100g) hank—approx 220yd (200m)—of deep pink (H)

US size 7 (4.5mm) crochet hook

Fabric to line bag

Sewing needle and thread

Tip
Only use 100% wool yarn for the flowers or they will not felt.

Abbreviations

beg beginning
ch chain
cont continue
dc double crochet
foll following
rem remaining
rep repeat
RS right side
sc single crochet
sp space
ss slip stitch
st(s) stitch(es)
tr treble
WS wrong side
yo yarn over hook

Special abbreviation

trCL (treble cluster) yo twice, insert yarn in sp, pull yarn through work, yo, pull yarn through 2 loops (3 loops on hook), *yo twice, insert hook in same sp, pull yarn through work, yo, pull yarn through 2 loops (5 loops on hook); rep from * twice (9 loops on hook), yo, pull yarn through all 9 loops on hook, 1ch (1 trCL made)

Gauge

Each square measures 4¼in. (11cm) square using US size 7 (4.5mm) hook.

Finished measurements

Approx 16½ x 13¾in. (41.5 x 35cm)

Front & Back panel

(make 12 squares, 2 in each contrast color for Round 2)

Using A, make 6ch, join with ss in first ch to form a ring.

Round 1: 4ch (counts as first tr), 11tr in ring, join with ss in top of first 4-ch. (12 tr)

Fasten off A. Join contrast color in first sp.

Round 2: 4ch, yo twice, insert yarn in first sp, pull yarn through work, yo, pull yarn through 2 loops (3 loops on hook), *yo twice, insert hook in same sp, pull yarn through work, yo, pull yarn through 2 loops (5 loops on hook); rep from * once more (7 loops on hook), yo, pull through all 7 loops, 1ch (counts as first trCL), 1trCL in the next and each sp to end of round, join with a ss in top of first trCL. (12 trCL)

Fasten off contrast color. Join A in any ch sp.

Round 3: 4ch (counts as first tr), [2tr, 3ch, 3tr] in same sp, *[3tr in next sp] twice, [3tr, 3ch, 3tr] in next sp; rep from * twice more, [3tr in next sp] twice, join with ss in top of first 4-ch.

Round 4: 1ch, *1sc in each st to corner, 3sc in corner ch sp, rep from * 3 times more, 1sc in each st, join with ss in first sc.

Fasten off.

Take one of each pair of squares and join in two horizontal rows of three using sc seam on RS. Fasten off after joining each pair of squares and leave center of 3-sc unjoined where the 4 squares meet. Rep with rem squares, so front and back panels of bag are the same.

Panel base:

Mark top and bottom of each panel. Working on bottom edge of first panel with RS facing, join A in center st of 3-sc at first corner, *1sc in each of next 14 sc, 1sc in seam; rep from * once more, 1sc in each of next 15 sc along last square. (46 sts)

Fasten off A. Attach B in first st.

Work all rows with RS facing.

Row 1: 3ch (counts as first dc), 2dc in same st, 1ch, * skip 2 sts, 3dc in next st; rep from * to end.

Fasten off B. Attach C at beg of last row between first 3-ch and first st.

Row 2: 3ch, 3dc in next and each sp, ending 3dc in last sp, 3ch, ss in top of last 3-dc from previous row.

Fasten off C. Attach D in first 3-ch sp at beg of previous row.

Row 3: 3ch, 2dc in same sp, 3dc in next and each sp, ending 3dc in last ch sp.

Fasten off D.

Rep Row 2 using E and Row 3 using F, then rep Row 2 again using G.

Fasten off.

Rep for second panel.

Bag Sides & Bottom

Using B, make 164ch.
Row 1: 1sc in 2nd ch from hook, 1sc in each ch to end. (163 sts)
Row 2: 1ch, 1sc in each st to end.
Fasten off B, attach A.
Row 3: 1ch, 1sc in each st to end.
Fasten off A, attach C.
Row 4: 1ch, 1sc in each st to end.
Row 5: 1ch, 1sc in each st to end.
Fasten off C, attach A.
Rows 6–26: Rep Rows 3–5, always working Row 3 in A and working Rows 4 and 5 in the foll order: D, F, E, G, B, C, and D.
Fasten off.

Handles

(make 2)
Using B, make 107ch.
Row 1: 1sc in 2nd ch from hook, 1sc in each ch to end. (106 sts)
Row 2: 1ch, 1sc in each st to end.
Fasten off B, attach C.
Rep Row 2, changing color every 2 rows in same order as bag sides and bottom (not using A), until a total of 12 rows have been worked.
Fasten off.

Finishing

Before joining, use front and back panels, together with bag sides and bottom, as a guide to cut fabric for lining, allowing an extra 2in. (5cm) for top edging, plus ½in. (1cm) extra all around for seams. Allowing ½in. (1cm) extra all around for seams, cut fabric lining for handles.
Mark center of each side of sides & bottom piece. Mark center of each panel base. With RS facing, match marks and pin sides & bottom piece to base and sides of each panel. Join with sc seam on WS.

Top edging:
Round 1: Using A and with RS facing, join yarn in top right-hand corner of end square. 1sc in each st across first 3 squares, 1sc in each st across first side panel, 1sc in each st across second 3 squares, 1sc in each st across side panel, join with a ss in first sc.
Cont making 1sc in each st around until edging measures 2in. (5cm).
Fasten off.

Lining

With RS together, sew bag lining pieces together, leaving top open. Handstitch handle lining to WS of each handle, turning raw edges under as you work. Sew handles to top of top edging of bag to align with corner edge of squares. Push fabric lining in bag, WS together, and handstitch lining to bag around top opening, turning raw edges under as you work.

Flowers

(make 6)
Using H, make 5ch, join with ss to make a ring.
Round 1: *1sc, 1dc, 1sc in ring; rep from * 3 more times. (4 petals)
Round 2: *2ch, from WS ss in base of 2nd sc of next petal (pick up 2 loops); rep from * 3 more times, ss in first 2-ch. (4 loops)
Round 3: *4dc in next 2-ch sp at back, ss in same ch sp; rep from * 3 more times.
Fasten off.
Place flowers in washing machine on 60ºC wash. Allow to dry naturally. Sew flowers spaced along top edge of bag.

BLOCK COLOR PILLOW

skill level

THE LOOPED EDGES OF THIS PILLOW GIVE IT SOME MOVEMENT, WHILE THE COLORS WILL MAKE A FASHION STATEMENT ON YOUR SOFA.

MATERIALS

50% baby alpaca/50% merino wool mix worsted (Aran) yarn, such as Rooster Almerino Aran

>> 1 x 1¾oz (50g) ball—approx 103yd (94m)—each of pale yellow (A), aquamarine (B), off-white (C), bright pink (D)

55% merino/33% microfiber/12% cashmere worsted (Aran) yarn, such as Debbie Bliss Cashmerino Aran

>> 1 x 1¾oz (50g) ball—approx 98.5yd (90m)—of black (E)

US size 7 (4.5mm) crochet hook

Yarn sewing needle

16-in. (40-cm) square pillow form

Abbreviations

ch chain
hdc half double crochet
rep repeat
RS right side
sc single crochet
st(s) stitches
ss slip stitch
WS wrong side
yo yarn over hook

Special abbreviations

Loop St with yarn over left index finger, insert hook in next st, draw 2 strands through st (take first strand from under index finger and at same time take 2nd strand from over index finger), pull yarn to tighten loop forming 1in (2.5cm) loop on index finger. Remove finger from loop, put loop to back (RS) of work, yo, and pull through 3 loops on hook (1 loop st made on RS)

Gauge

15 hdc x 12 rows over 4in. (10cm) square working hdc using US size 7 (4.5mm) hook.

Finished measurement

Fits 16-in (40-cm) square pillow form

Pillow

(make 2 pieces the same)

Using A, make 63ch.

Row 1 (RS): 1hdc in 2nd ch from hook, 1hdc in each ch to end. (62 sts)

Row 2: 2ch (counts as 1hdc), 1hdc in each st to end. (62 sts)

Rep Row 2 eight times more.

Fasten off A, attach E.

Work Row 2 once.

Fasten off E, attach B.

Work Row 2 fifteen times.

Fasten off B, attach E.

Work Row 2 once.

Fasten off E, attach C.

Work Row 2 thirteen times.

Fasten off C, attach E.

Work Row 2 once.

Fasten off E, attach D.

Work Row 2 eight times.

Fasten off.

Finishing

With WS together and using E, join bottom and two sides using sc seam working 2sc in each corner and leaving top open. Insert pillow form. Close top using sc seam. Fasten off.

Edging

With WS facing, join E in first st after corner along top.

Round 1 (WS facing): 1ch, work Loop St in each st, join with a ss in first st. Fasten off.

Round 2 (WS facing): Join E in first st, rep Round 1. Fasten off.

- » Holding the hook
- » Holding the yarn
- » Making a slip knot
- » Yarn over hook (yo)
- » Chain (ch)
- » Single crochet (sc)
- » Half double crochet (hdc)
- » Double crochet (dc)
- » Treble (tr)
- » Double treble (dtr)
- » Triple treble (trtr)
- » Chain space (ch sp)
- » Making rows
- » Making rounds

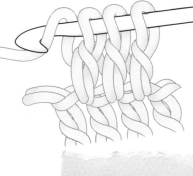

Double 3 stitches together

Treble

- » Decreasing
- » Single crochet 2 stitches together (sc2tog)
- » Single crochet 3 stitches together (sc3tog)
- » Half double 2 stitches together (hdc2tog)
- » Double 3 stitches together (dc3tog)
- » Treble 2 stitches together (tr2tog)
- » Treble 3 stitches together (tr3tog)
- » Increasing

CROCHET KNOW-HOW

Increasing

Cluster

TECHNIQUES

IN THIS SECTION, WE EXPLAIN HOW TO MASTER THE SIMPLE CROCHET TECHNIQUES THAT YOU NEED TO MAKE THE PROJECTS IN THIS BOOK.

• •

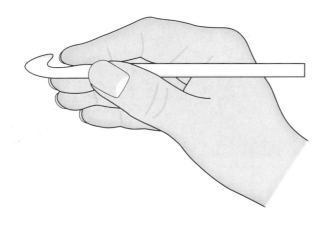

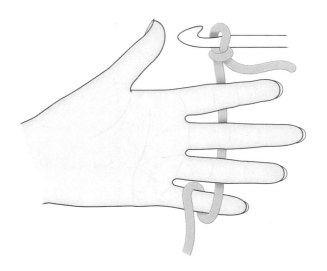

Holding the hook

Pick up your hook as though you are picking up a pen or pencil. Keeping the hook held loosely between your fingers and thumb, turn your hand so that the palm is facing up and the hook is balanced in your hand and resting in the space between your index finger and your thumb.

Holding the yarn

Pick up the yarn with your little finger in the opposite hand to your hook, with your palm facing upward. Turn your hand to face downward, with the yarn on top of your index finger and under the other two fingers and wrapped right around the little finger. Keeping your index finger only at a slight curve, hold your work just under the slip knot with the other hand.

Making a slip knot

The simplest way is to make a circle with the yarn, so that the loop is facing downward.

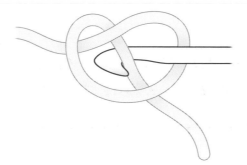

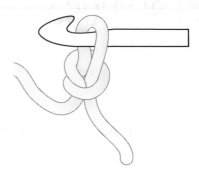

1 In one hand hold the circle at the top, where the yarn crosses, and let the tail drop down so that it falls in the center of the loop. With your free hand or the tip of a crochet hook, pull the tail through the loop and pull the knot, so that it tightens loosely.

2 Put the hook into the circle and pull the knot gently so that it forms a loose loop on the hook.

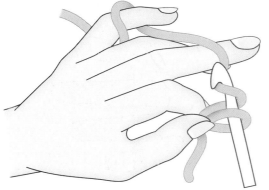

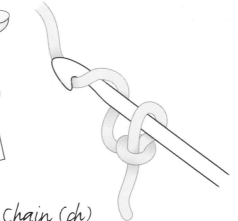

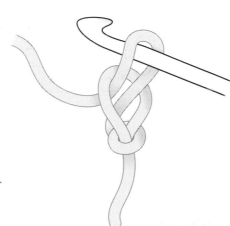

Yarn over hook (yo)

To create a stitch, you'll need to catch the yarn with the hook and pull it through the loop. Holding your yarn and hook correctly, catch the yarn from behind with the hook pointed upward. As you gently pull the yarn through the loop on the hook, turn the hook so that it faces downward and slide the yarn through the loop. The loop on the hook should be kept loose enough for the hook to slide through easily.

Chain (ch)

1 Using the hook, wrap the yarn over the hook and pull it through the loop on the hook, creating a new loop on the hook. Continue in this way to create a chain of the required length.

2 Keep moving your middle finger and thumb close to the hook, to hold the work in place with the opposite hand that you hold your hook with.

single crochet (sc)

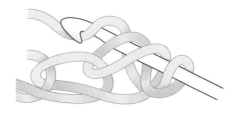 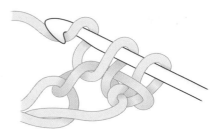

1 Insert the hook into your work, yarn over hook, and pull the yarn through the work. You will then have two loops on the hook.

2 Yarn over hook again and pull through the two loops on the hook. You will then have one loop on the hook.

Half double crochet (hdc)

  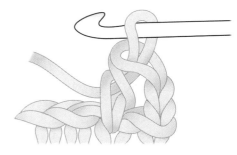

1 Before inserting the hook into the work, wrap the yarn over the hook and put the hook through the work with the yarn wrapped around.

2 Yarn over hook again and pull through the first loop on the hook (you now have three loops on the hook).

3 Yarn over hook and pull the yarn through all three loops. You will be left with one loop on the hook.

Double crochet (dc)

1 Before inserting the hook into the work, wrap the yarn over the hook and put the hook through the work with the yarn wrapped around.

2 Yarn over hook again and pull through the first loop on the hook (you now have three loops on the hook). Yarn over hook again, pull the yarn through two loops (you now have two loops on the hook).

3 Pull the yarn through two loops again. You will be left with one loop on the hook.

Treble (tr)

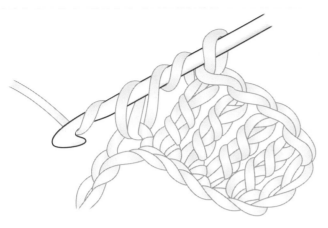

Yarn over hook twice, insert hook into the stitch, yarn over hook, pull a loop through (four loops on hook), yarn over hook, pull the yarn through two stitches (three loops on hook), yarn over hook, pull a loop through the next two stitches (two loops on hook), yarn over hook, pull a loop through the last two stitches.

Double treble (dtr)

Yarn over hook three times, insert hook into the stitch, yarn over hook, pull a loop through (five loops on hook), yarn over hook, pull the yarn through two stitches (four loops on hook), yarn over hook, pull a loop through the next two stitches (three loops on hook), yarn over hook, pull a loop through the next two stitches (two loops on hook), yarn over hook, pull a loop through the last two stitches.

Triple treble (trtr)

For trtr, begin by wrapping the yarn over the hook four times and then proceed in the same way as for double treble (above) until you are left with one loop on the hook.

Chain space (ch sp)

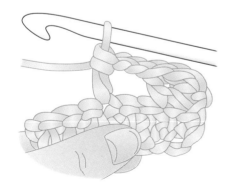

1 A chain space is the space that has been made under a chain in the previous round or row, and falls in between other stitches.

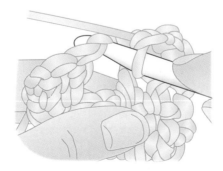

2 Stitches into a chain space are made directly into the hole created under the chain and not into the chain stitches themselves.

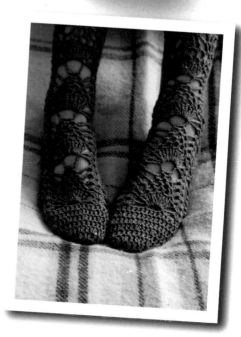

Making rows

When making straight rows, you need to make a turning chain to create the height you need for the stitch you are working with, as follows:

Single crochet = 1 chain
Half double crochet = 2 chain
Double crochet = 3 chain
Treble = 4 chain
Double treble = 5 chain
Triple treble = 6 chain

Making rounds

When working in rounds the work is not turned, so you are always working from one side. Depending on the pattern you are working, a "round" can be square. Again, you will need to make a turning chain to create the height you need for the stitch you are working, as listed under making rows (left).

To keep count of where you are in the pattern, you will need to place a stitch marker at the beginning of each round; a piece of yarn in a contrasting color is useful for this. Loop the stitch marker into the first stitch; when you have made a round and reached the point where the stitch marker is, work this stitch, take out the stitch marker from the previous round, and put it back into the first stitch of the new round.

Decreasing

You can decease either by missing the next stitch and continuing to crochet or by crocheting two or more stitches together. The basic technique for crocheting stitches together is the same, no matter which stitch you are using.

single crochet 2 stitches together (sc2tog)

 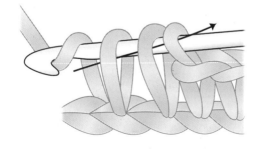

1 Insert the hook into your work, yarn over hook, and pull the yarn through the work. You will then have two loops on the hook.

2 Yarn over hook again and pull through the two loops on the hook. You will then have one loop on the hook.

single crochet 3 stitches together (sc3tog)

Work as for sc2tog until there are three loops on the hook; insert hook into the next st, yarn over hook, pull yarn through (four loops on hook), yarn over hook and pull through all the loops; one loop left on the hook.

Half double crochet 2 stitches together (hdc2tog)

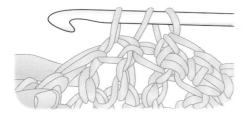  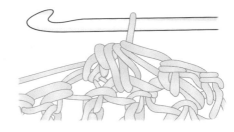

1 Yarn over hook, insert hook into next stitch, yarn over hook, draw yarn through (three loops on hook).

2 Yarn over hook, insert hook into next stitch, yarn over hook, draw yarn through.

3 Draw yarn through all five loops on hook.

Double crochet 3 stitches together (dc3tog)

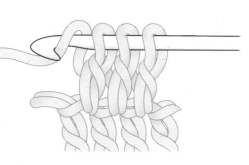

Work a double into each of the next three stitches as normal, but leave the last loop of each stitch on the hook (four loops on the hook). Yarn over hook and pull the yarn through all the stitches on the hook to join them together. You will finish with one loop on the hook.

Treble 2 stitches together (tr2tog)

Yarn over hook twice, insert hook into st (or as directed in pattern), pull yarn through (four loops on hook), pull yarn through two loops (three loops on hook), yarn over hook twice, insert hook into st (or as directed in pattern), pull yarn through (six loops on hook), pull yarn through two loops (five loops on hook),* pull yarn through all five loops (one loop on hook).

Treble 3 stitches together (dtr3tog)

Work as for tr2tog (above) to *, yarn over hook twice, insert the hook into the stitch (or as directed in pattern), pull yarn through (eight loops on hook), pull yarn through two loops (seven loops on hook), pull yarn through all seven loops (one loop on the hook).

Increasing

Make two or three stitches into one stitch from the previous row. The illustration shows a two-stitch increase being made.

Fastening off

Cut the yarn, leaving a tail of approx 4in. (10cm). Pull the tail all the way through the last loop.

How to single crochet squares together

Place two squares wrong sides together, lining them up so that the stitches on each square match. Put the hook through the top loops of the first square and also through the corresponding top loops of the second square. Join in the yarn, make 1 chain, insert the hook into the top stitches of both squares, and make a single crochet seam across the top of the squares.

Cluster

Working two or more part stitches and taking them together at the top to make one stitch gives a decrease when working a fabric or a cluster in a stitch pattern. The example shows decreasing by taking three doubles together.

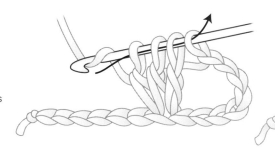

1 Leaving the last loop of each stitch on the hook, work a double into each of the next three stitches, thus making four loops on the hook.

2 Yarn over hook and pull through all four loops to join the stitches together at the top and make one loop on hook.

Popcorn

This kind of bobble is made from complete stitches. The example shows five doubles worked in a chain space and taken together, but a popcorn can be placed in any stitch and be made up of any practical number or combination of stitches.

1 Inserting the hook in the same place each time, work five complete doubles.

2 Slip the hook out of the last loop.

3 Insert the hook into the top of the first stitch, then into the last loop, yarn over hook, and pull through.

Loop stitch

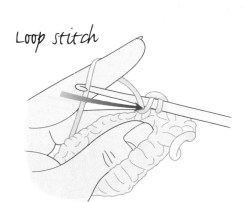

1 With the yarn over the left index finger, insert the hook into the next stitch and draw two strands through the stitch (take the first strand from under the index finger and at the same time take the second strand from over the index finger).

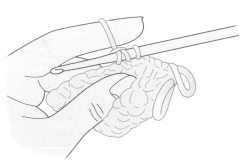

2 Pull the yarn to tighten the loop, forming a 1-in. (2.5-cm) loop on the index finger. Remove finger from the loop, put the loop to the back of the work, yarn over hook, and pull through three loops on the hook (1 loop stitch made on right side of work).

Intarsia

Use small balls of wool; one each side of the motif, and one or more for the motif. Use the background color to one stitch before the motif; change color by bringing in the motif color on the last pull through of the stitch. Crochet the motif stitch(es) as per the chart; one stitch before the end of the motif change to the background color in the same way. Keep color changes to the wrong side of the work.

SUPPLIERS

The yarns used in these projects should be available from your local yarn or craft store. If you can't find the correct yarn, try some of the websites listed here.

WEB SITES

Laughing Hens
www.laughinghens.com

Debbie Bliss
www.debbieblissonline.com

Coats Crafts Rowan Yarns
www.coatscrafts.co.uk

Purl Soho
www.purlsoho.com

Yarn Forward
www.yarnforward.com

Fyberspates
www.fyberspates.co.uk

US STOCKISTS

Wool2Dye4
6000-K Boonsboro Road
Coffee Crossing
Lynchburg
VA 24503
www.wool2dye4.com

Knitting Fever
Stockists of Debbie Bliss, Noro, and Sirdar yarns
www.knittingfever.com

The Knitting Garden
Stockists of Rowan yarns
www.theknittinggarden.com

Lets Knit
www.letsknit.com

Webs
www.yarn.com

Yarn Market
www.yarnmarket.com

Unicorn Books and Crafts
www.unicornbooks.com

A.C. Moore
Stores nationwide
1-888-226-6673
www.acmoore.com

Crafts, etc.
Online store
1-800-888-0321
www.craftsetc.com

Hobby Lobby
Stores nationwide
www.hobbylobby.com

Jo-Ann Fabric and Craft Store
Stores nationwide
1-888-739-4120
www.joann.com

Michaels
Stores nationwide
1-800-642-4235
www.michaels.com

UK STOCKISTS

Laughing Hens
(wool, hooks, accessories)
The Croft Stables
Station Lane
Great Barrow
Cheshire CH3 7JN
01829 740903
www.laughinghens.com

Fyberspates
Unit 6 Oxleaze Farm Workshops
Broughton Poggs
Filkins
Lechlade
Glos GL7 3RB
07540 656660
www.fyberspates.co.uk

Rooster Yarns
Laughing Hens online
Wool, patterns, knitting, & crochet supplies
Online.
www.laughinghens.com
01829 740903

Debbie Bliss Yarns
Designer Yarns
Units 8–10 Newbridge Industrial Estate
Pitt Street, Keighley
West Yorkshire BD21 4PA
01535 664222
www.designeryarns.uk.com

Rowan Yarns
Green Lane Mill
Holmfirth
West Yorkshire HD9 2DX
01484 681881
www.knitrowan.com

John Lewis
Stores nationwide
0845 604 9049
www.johnlewis.com

TUITION

Nicki Trench Workshops
Crochet, knitting, patchwork, quilting,
and sewing workshops for all levels
Email: nicki@nickitrench.com

INDEX

ACKNOWLEDGMENTS

• •

Writing this book has involved far more people than usual and I'm totally indebted to everyone who has contributed to getting it to publication.

I'm particularly grateful to Sian Brown, who helped me hugely with the specs, designs, and crocheters and whom without I don't think I would have got the projects completed.

Thanks also to Duriye Foley, who always goes the extra mile. Other crocheters and pattern writers that I'm extremely grateful to are: Awatif Aljabry, Tash Bentley, Pat Cooper, Holly Gunning, Penny Hill, Judith Isaacs, Emma Jamieson, Emma Lightfoot, Sue Lumsden, Carolyn Meggison, Beryl Oakes, Sophia Reed, Jenny Shore, Rita Taylor, Fran Wensel, Jenny Shore, and Janet Vowles.

Thanks to the boys at Laughing Hens, Andy Robinson and Johnny Okell, who always responded to my urgent pleas for yarn at a moment's notice and who donated all the Rooster yarns for free; also thanks to Ian at Designer Yarns for donating the Debbie Bliss yarn and getting it to me so efficiently.

Thanks to Cindy Richards at Cico Books for her great insight in commissioning this book; to Pete Jorgensen who is always patient, forgiving, and a great support throughout the writing process. Also to Marie Clayton for her brilliant editing, to Susan Horan for all her hard work in the pattern-checking process, and to my mum, who expertly untangled patterns and helped make some of the projects.

Finally, I really owe my biggest thanks to my daughters, Camilla and Maddy, for helping make some sense of the current vintage fashion and guiding me through the wonderful world of the East London trend I was aiming for. Girls—this is dedicated to you; you are great.